Paleo DIET Cookbook

250+ Essentials Paleo recipes to Lose weight and Tone Your Body to the Top! Reboot your Health with a 21-Day Beginners Meal Plan!

Simon James

INTRODUCTION...3

ADVANTAGES OF PALEO DIET 4

BREAKFAST RECIPES 7

PALEO LUNCH RECIPES 17

VERY HEALTHY RECIPES FOR DINNER..28

FRESH PALEO MEAT RECIPES 40

PALEO DESSERTS AND SNACKS 48

STRONG PALEO SOUPS, STEWS AND CHILIES...70

DELICIOUS SALAD RECIPES..80

EVENT AND SPECIAL OCCASION PALEO-MEALS 85

21-DAY MEAL PLAN 97

CONCLUSION...98

Introduction

Paleo diet is basically all about a version of a specific diet that aids in shedding weight and reducing various types of chronic conditions. **The basic premise of this diet is to consume foods that can help an individual achieve optimum health.** This diet is based on the foods that were consumed mainly by the pre-historic Stone-Age people, so encourages the consumption of foods that are naturally grown and purely natural. Eating processed foods is absolutely forbidden in this diet: Paleo diet does not encourage the consumption of artificial additives, preservatives, sweeteners, coloring, artificial flavors, and chemical processes that are physically impossible to avoid. **All the ingredients used in this diet must be grown without using the aid of any chemical approaches.** The basic premise of this diet is completely on the replacement of processed foods with high fiber foods that are rich in soluble minerals and vitamins. Why could the Paleo Diet be good for you? This diet is completely focused on natural food, so your organism will produce fewer toxins and work better. **Do you know anything that it is better than eating completely natural foods?** I think it isn't easy. Moreover, **the reduction of carbohydrates is a fundamental principle of Paleo Diet**, so it can help you in **weight loss!** Scientific Researches discovered that following a low-carbohydrate and high-protein diet is regarded as one of the best ways to prevent cardiovascular diseases by overcoming digestive problems and increasing metabolic rates and fat burning. For this reason, I think a diet like Paleo Diet can be entirely adopted by every person who wants to maintain high healthy level, especially after a stressfully situation as days of busy job or fasting too. Following the Paleo diet is very simple, because it is based on the caveman food. You only need to follow the principle of eating vegetables considered in the diet and need to start with steamed vegetables and a source of fruits to eat. There is no limitation for the types of fruits to eat: you can use in your meals a lot of varieties of fruits which are rich in vitamins and minerals, including figs, pineapples, apples, blueberries, bananas and many others. **In this book, you will find 250+ fantastic recipes, you can organize your cooking, even if you are very busy!**   **Let's read together!**

Advantages of Paleo Diet

Paleo diet has several advantages over other diets, some of which we'll discuss here:

Easy to Follow, Satisfying, and Filling

Thanks to the nature of the diet, it is easier to follow, and just about anyone from young to old can benefit from it. This is why the Paleo Diet is growing in popularity nowadays. The Paleo diet is one that is simple and doesn't require a lot of thought. The main purpose of this diet is to offer nourishment for the body by giving it back the nutrients that it is lacking in. In addition, this diet is also very satisfying and filling. Most of the people who have tried this diet have always been very happy with it because it provides them with great satisfaction and helps them burn a lot of calories in the process.

People Who Start Paleo Diet Found It Difficult to Get Back into Their Old Diet Habits

The Paleo diet restricts the intake of a lot of carbohydrates and fruits. Therefore, people who have ditched the Paleo diet will find it hard to get back into the old diet habits. The reason for this is that it takes time for the body to get back in the groove of the normal diet. That said, once you get started, you will be able to stick to it easily. As with anything else, it takes time getting used to a new diet and lifestyle. If you stick to it without giving up, you can be sure that you'll start to enjoy the many benefits that come from it. With Paleo diet, you are sure to shed more weight and be healthier and feel better in general. Paleo diet is also a lot easier to stick to than the older diets out there. This is because this diet doesn't require one to eat at certain intervals of the day or count calories. In fact, one of the main advantages of this diet is that it allows you to eat as much as you want, as long as you get the right foods from the right sources. You just have to avoid the foods that aren't good for you and may cause a compromise to your health. When done right, this is a great advantage, as it is far less restrictive than other diets out there.

The Paleo Diet Is Ideal for Those Who Are Health Conscious

The idea of eating the foods that our ancestors used to eat is indeed a very attractive thought, because of the long list of health benefits that it has always been associated with. The real difficulty is knowing what the best foods for us are to eat in order to get that health. However, since the Paleo diet prescribes you to eat the foods that our ancestors ate, then that means that you will get all the necessary vitamins and minerals that your body needs. Going back to the Paleo diet is a great way to guarantee that your body gets all the necessary vitamins and minerals it needs. This is a great advantage because while Paleo diet has a lot of health benefits, it is also very effective in relieving disease and other health ailments. As a matter of fact, it has been proven that this diet is capable of preventing and even curing a lot of health problems. With this diet, you won't die from diabetes or any other deadly disease, which is a great advantage in itself. Since it works towards alleviating health problems and eliminating any potential health risks out there, one can very well say that the Paleo diet is a much better diet option than the other types of diets out there. Paleo diet is a great option for those who are very health conscious. You will be very pleased to know that this diet is also full of great have a much better and safer life when you follow this diet. There are many people out there who have said that they have greatly reduced the risk of having many health complications even before they follow the diet. So, it is clear that most Paleo dieters are very satisfied with this diet and would highly recommend it to anyone who wants to be healthier and live a happy, healthier and safer life.

You Are Sure to Feel More Confident

By adhering to the Paleo diet, you can be sure that you'll end up eating more than what your body needs and because of this, you will start losing weight. With this kind of diet, it takes a lot of thought to learn, but once you get the hang of it, you will be able to lose weight quickly. With Paleo diet, you're sure to end up feeling more confident and productive. One of the main advantages of Paleo diet is that it is a complete diet that can be used by anyone no matter what their age is. This is because it is a very simple and easy diet to partake in. This is because with Paleo diet, you don't need to count the calories and make complicated plans to lose weight quickly. This is because you are sure to lose weight and gain a lot of energy and focus after following the Paleo diet. This diet is very convenient as it works on giving you the right amount of food you need to eat, and you can be sure that you will be able to stick to it easily once you get started. This is because there are no complicated things that you need to learn to make it work for you. Lastly, Paleo diet is great because it can be followed by anyone and everyone as it is simple and easy to do. It can be implemented by anyone at any time and it is one of the best diets that can be followed by anyone. With all of these advantages, you will be sure to carry a lot of energy with you and the confidence to do things properly. This is all because of the Paleo diet and it is thanks to these many health benefits that people can swallow the cost and effort that come with it.

WHAT CAN YOU EAT IN PALEO DIET?

Following, there is a guideline about foods you can eat or not in Paleo diet. Practically you should eat only unprocessed food such as fresh meats, vegetables, and fruits.

However, each people can adapt Paleo diet in his/her lifestyle. I think each diet should be an instrument in our life to have healthier and more wellness, not a "dogma": so, I agree with a less rigid and more flexible Paleo diet, with some little "exception". Then, in this book, I wanted to insert some recipes with some more refined ingredients, bordering the Paleo diet, to allow people to start the Paleo diet gradually!

However, following there are some foods you can eat in Paleo Diet

TUBERS AND ROOTS

▪ Beetroot	▪ Sweet Potatoes	▪ Topinambur	▪ Tigernut
▪ Daikon		▪ Chufa	▪ Cipero

VEGETABLES

▪ Agretti	▪ Brussel Spout	▪ Mushrooms	▪ Shallot
▪ Asparagus	▪ Cauliflower	▪ Salad	▪ Celery
▪ Basil	▪ Cabbage	▪ Eggplant	▪ Pumpkin
▪ Broccoli	▪ Cucumbers	▪ Radicchio	▪ Zucchini
▪ Artichokes	▪ Chicory	▪ Turnip	
▪ Carrots	▪ Onions	▪ Radish	

FISH

- Anchovy
- Bleak
- Alice
- Lobster
- Herring
- Squid
- Scallops
- Capitone
- Carp
- Cicerello
- Mussel
- Mollusk
- Gallinella
- Snapper
- Shrimp
- Crab
- Halibut
- Cod
- Moscardino
- Sea bream
- Oysters
- Palombo
- Perch
- Catfish
- Octopus
- Rhombus
- Salmon
- Sardine
- Sepia
- Emery
- Sole
- Sea bass
- Tuna
- Mullet
- Trout
- Clam

FRUIT

- Apricot
- Black cherry
- Pineapple
- Oranges
- Avocado
- Goji berries
- Bananas
- Cedar
- Cherries
- Coconut
- Watermelon
- Dates
- Kiwi
- Passion fruit
- Strawberries
- Lime
- Lemon
- Mango
- Apple
- Pomegranate
- Papaya
- Tamarind
- Currants
- Grapes

EGGS
FLOURS

- Banana Flour
- Chestnut Flour
- Coconut Flour
- Almond Flour
- Chufa Flour
- Hemp Flour
- Sweet potato Flour

OILS AND FATS

- Coconut oil
- Ghee
- Duck fat
- Coconut milk
- Avocado oil
- Linseed oil
- Almond oil
- Hazelnut oil
- Walnut oil
- Red Palm oil
- Fish oil
- Pumpkin seed oil
- Bacon
- Lard

MEAT

- Lamb
- Duck
- Bison
- Buffalo
- Capon
- Goat
- Roe deer
- Horse
- Rabbit
- Hen
- Hare
- Pig
- Beef
- Goose
- Pigeon
- Chicken
- Turkey
- Game
- Animal Organs

MILK

- Coconut Milk
- Kefir Milk
- Almond milk
- Hazelnut milk

SEEDS AND NUTS

- Cashew
- Chestnuts
- Almonds
- Hazelnuts
- Walnuts
- Brazilian nuts
- Pecan nuts
- Pistachios
- Flax seeds
- Sesame seeds
- Pumpkin seeds
- Chia seeds

Breakfast Recipes

1. Super Moroccan Lemon Beef Stew

Preparation Time: 20 minutes
Cooking Time: 4 hours
Servings: 4 to 6
Ingredients:

- 1 medium butternut squash (Diced)
- Pinch of salt and pepper, each
- 3 medium yellow onions (Diced)
- 1/3 cup butter
- 3 garlic cloves (Minced)
- Juice from 2 lemons
- 2 ½ tablespoons raselhanout spice
- 2 cups beef broth
- 2 pounds stewing beef

Directions:

1. Place all the ingredients but the squash in the slow cooker.
2. Cover and cook properly on medium for about 3 to 4 hours, until meat is tender.
3. Add the squash to the cooker; then cook properly for another hour.
4. Finally serve in bowls, over rice.

2. Great Garlic mushrooms with bacon

Preparation Time: 10 minutes
Cooking Time: 15 to 20 minutes
Servings: 2 to 3 portions
Ingredients:

- 3 bacon rashers
- Pinch salt and pepper
- 3 garlic cloves
- 2 ½ tablespoons chopped parsley
- 3 tablespoons olive oil
- 210g Portobello mushrooms

Directions:

1. Pre-heat a grill pan over medium-high heat, pour olive oil.
2. Apart from, wash mushrooms, dry them with paper towels, slice. Dice bacon rashers, chop garlic cloves and mix them with sliced mushrooms in a bowl. Put all the ingredients in the grill pan. Fry for about 5 to 10 minutes, stirring from time to time.
3. Finally transfer to the plates, add salt and pepper, decorate with chopped parsley.

3. Happy Delicious Glazed Carrots

Preparation Time: 10 to 15 minutes
Cooking Time: 3 to 4 hours
Servings: 8 to 9
Ingredients:

- 3/4 cup of water
- A pinch of nutmeg, ground
- ½ cup raw honey
- 1 teaspoon cinnamon, ground
- A pinch of sea salt
- 2 pounds carrots (Sliced)

Directions:

1. Put carrots in your slow cooker.
2. Add water, salt, raw honey, cinnamon and nutmeg, toss well, cover and cook properly on high heat

for about 2 to 3 hours.

3. Finally stir again, divide between plates and serve as a side dish.

4. Lucky Quinoa Veggie Breakfast Bowl

Preparation Time: 15 minutes

Cooking Time: 20 minutes

Servings: 3

Ingredients:

- Salt and pepper
- ½ cup of water
- ½ cup broccoli (Chopped)
- ½ cup of Coconut milk
- ½ cup of sliced mushrooms
- 1 egg
- ½ cup quinoa, rinsed

Directions:

1. Add olive oil to a skillet set over medium heat. Add mushrooms and broccoli and stir-fry for about 5 to 10 minutes or until cooked through. Remove the skillet from heat and set aside.
2. In a saucepan, combine water, quinoa, and coconut milk; bring to a gentle boil and lower heat to low. Then simmer until almost all liquid is absorbed.
3. Stir in veggies, cheese, and salt and pepper until well combined. Cover and set aside.
4. Fry the egg sunny side up. Finally serve quinoa in a bowl topped with the egg.

5. Vintage Zucchini and Sweet Potato (Fritatta)

Preparation Time: 5 to 10 minutes

Cooking Time: 20 to 25 minutes

Servings: 2 to 4

Ingredients:

- Fresh parsley – 1 tablespoon
- Pepper and salt to taste
- Eggs – 8
- 1 cutted, peeled large sweet potato
- Red bell pepper – 1 (Sliced)
- Sliced zucchini – 2
- 2 ½ tablespoons Butter or coconut oil

Directions:

1. Add oil to a cooking pan then heat over medium heat, then add the slices of sweet potato and cook properly for about 5 to 10 minutes. Add red bell pepper and zucchini slices.
2. Continue cooking for about 2 to 5 minutes. While still cooking, whisk the eggs into a bowl.
3. Season the egg with pepper and salt; add to the vegetables.
4. Cook properly over low heat for about 10 to 15 minutes then in a heated broiler allow the frittata to become golden.
5. Finally cut the frittata into pieces then have it served with fresh parsley.

6. Best Butternut Squash and Kale Beef Stew

Preparation Time: 35 minutes

Cooking Time: 55 minutes

Servings: 8 to 10

Ingredients:

- 2 lb. stew beef, 1" cubed
- Salt and pepper
- 1 onion, roughly chopped
- 4 cups beef stock, preferably homemade
- 4 garlic cloves (Minced)

- 16oz frozen, chopped kale
- 1 ½ tablespoon fresh sage (Minced)
- ½ tsp paprika
- 4 cups butternut squash, cubed
- 2 ½ tablespoons bacon fat

Directions:

1. In a slow cook quickly heat 1 tbsp. bacon fat over medium high; then working in batches, brown the meat, making sure not to cook it properly through (it can turn tough). Set browned meat aside. Lower heat to medium and add the 2nd tbsp. bacon fat.
2. Once it's melted add the garlic, onions, smoked paprika, and sage to pot, along with a big pinch of salt and fresh pepper.
3. Cook properly about 5 to 10 minutes, or until the onions begin to soften and turn translucent.
4. Then make sure to stir frequently so the mixture doesn't burn.
5. Add the beef, butternut squash, and kale to the pot. Stir to combine.
6. Add the chicken stock and 2 cups of hot water.
7. Bring to a boil, then reduce to a simmer and let cook, covered, for at least an hour.
8. If it needs, let it stand about 40 to 45 minutes longer.

7. Delightful Double chocolate cookies

Preparation Time: 10 minutes
Cooking Time: 20 minutes
Servings: 24 to 26 cookies
Ingredients:

- 1 cup cocoa powder
- 1 pinch sea salt
- 1 egg
- 1 cup almond butter
- 1 tbsp coconut oil
- 50 g of crumbled walnuts

Directions:

1. Preheat oven to about 340 to 350° F.
2. Mix all the ingredients in a bowl. Next, line a large baking sheet with parchment paper.
3. Finally form the cookies with a tablespoon and bake them for about 10 to 15 minutes, until just cooked.

8. Crazy Paleo Chili Turkey Stew

Preparation Time: 30 Minutes
Cooking Time: 6 hours
Servings: 8 to 10
Ingredients:

- 3 garlic cloves (Minced)
- 15 ounces can tomato sauce
- 1 ½ large onion (Diced)
- 28-ounce jar crushed tomatoes
- Red and green peppers (Diced)
- 1 stalk of celery (Diced)
- 14-ounce jar diced tomatoes
- 2 carrots (Diced)

- 1 ½ jalapeno pepper, diced

- 2 pounds ground turkey

Directions:

1. Sauté garlic and onion in a pot. Add onion, garlic with rest of ingredients to the pot.
2. Put the lid and cook on low for about 5 to 6 hours. Stir frequently.
3. Serve hot. Garnish with avocado.

9. Fantastic Gingersnaps

Preparation Time: 15 minutes
Cooking Time: 15 to 20 minutes
Servings: 24 to 26 cookies
Ingredients:

- 1 egg
- 1 pinch of sea salt
- About 2.5 tbsps. raw honey
- ¼ tsp freshly ground nutmeg
- 2 teaspoons powdered ginger
- About ½ tsp ground cloves
- 1 tsp cinnamon

- 1 cup almond butter

Directions:

1. Preheat oven to about 340 to 350 °F.
2. Mix all the ingredients in a bowl; then quickly line a large baking sheet with a parchment paper.
3. Finally form the cookies with a tablespoon and bake them for about 10 to 15 minutes, until just cooked.

10. Nostalgic Mustard Crusted Salmon with Arugula and Spinach Salad

Preparation Time: 15 to 20 Minutes
Cooking Time: 20 to 30 Minutes
Servings: 1 to 3
Ingredients:
FOR SALMON:

- About 1.5 tbsp. coarse ground mustard
- 15 oozes salmon filet
- A pinch of sea salt

FOR SALAD:

- About 2.5 tbsps. chopped pecans
- 1 cup chopped arugula
- 1/2 cup chopped baby spinach
- 2 tbsps. Dried cranberries

FOR DRESSING:

- About 1.5 tbsp. extra virgin olive oil
- 1 tbsp. Dijon mustard

Directions:

1. Preheat your oven to about 340 to 350°F.
2. Grease a baking sheet with extra virgin olive oil and place in salmon filet; pat dry with paper towels and sprinkle with ground mustard, covering the entire top if fish.
3. This step is important. Bake for about 15 to 20 minutes or until fish flakes easily with a fork.

4. Meanwhile, whisk together the dressing ingredients and set aside.
5. Then combine together the salad ingredients in a mixing bowl; add in the dressing and toss until well coated. Spoon your salad onto a serving bowl and top with salmon.
6. While the salmon is cooking, whisk together the ingredients for the dressing. Set aside.

11. Mighty Spicy Red Fish Stew

Preparation Time: 15 Minutes
Cooking Time: 30 Minutes
Servings: 3
Ingredients:

- 1 tablespoon olive oil
- Sea salt and pepper to taste
- 1 jar red bell peppers, chopped
- 1 teaspoon fresh lemon zest
- 8-10-ounce cod or halibut, fillets, cut into 1-inch pieces
- 2 cups diced tomatoes with juice
- 1 ½ teaspoon minced fresh garlic
- 2 teaspoons fresh lemon juice
- ¼ teaspoon red pepper flakes
- ¼ cup chopped fresh cilantro
- ½ cup finely chopped red onion

Directions:

1. Chop red onion or shallot. Drain and chop red bell peppers. Dice tomatoes and finely mince garlic. Add olive oil to a small, deep frying pan and heat over medium heat. Add onion and cook properly for about 2 to 5 minutes, until soft. Add red bell peppers, garlic, tomatoes with juice, and red pepper flakes. Then increase heat to medium-high and simmer for about 10 to 15 minutes. Meanwhile, zest the lemon and squeeze the juice.
2. Chop cilantro. Cut fish fillets into 1-inch pieces. Stir into the stew lemon zest and juice and cilantro. Add fish and carefully mix it in.
3. Next, simmer for about 5 to 10 more minutes; then stir the stew and taste.
4. Add salt and pepper as desired and serve hot, garnished with chopped cilantro.

12. King sized Waffles

Preparation Time: 20 Minutes
Cooking Time: 35 Minutes
Servings: 4
Ingredients:

- 1 carrot
- 1 ½ teaspoon vanilla extract
- 3 eggs
- ¼ cup coconut oil
- 2/3 cup coconut milk
- 1 egg
- 1 teaspoon baking soda
- 1 ½ teaspoon cinnamon
- 2/3 cup almond or coconut flour

Directions:

1. Heat up the coconut milk and dissolve the baking soda and leave to cool. While it is cooling, grate the carrot. Sift the flour into a bowl and add 2 eggs, the cinnamon, the grated carrot, and the milk/sodium. Mix together until the consistency resembles pancake batter. Next, let this entire mixture stand in a warm place while you make your cream mixture (which is optional).

2. <u>For the cream</u>: mix 1 egg, the vanilla, and the coconut oil until well incorporated, then quickly place in the refrigerator until it is time to eat the waffle. Pour the batter into a waffle iron and cook accordingly. Finally spoon some cream onto the waffle if made for the recipe and enjoy!

13. Pinnacle Dark chocolate mousse

Preparation Time: 10 Minutes
Cooking Time: 2 hour 20 minutes
Servings: 2 to 3 portions
Ingredients:

- ½ cup warm water
- 1 ½ teaspoon of honey
- 3 eggs
- ½ lb dark chocolate (85% cocoa solids or more)

Directions:

1. Break the chocolate and put it in a bowl with warm water; then put this bowl over a pot of simmering water (make sure the bowl doesn't touch the simmering water) and let the chocolate melt. Separate the eggs yolks and whites in 2 bowls.
2. Beat the yolks, add honey and whisk again.
3. When the chocolate is fully melted, remove it from the heat and let cool for about 2 to 5 minutes. Then beat the white to soft peaks.
4. Combine yolks with the chocolate, fold a tablespoon of the whites with a rubber spatula into the mixture, then carefully fold the rest of them.
5. Next, divide the mixture into 2 ramekins, cover with plastic wrap and put in the fridge for about 2.5 hours. Serve with coconut milk.

14. Perfect Scotch eggs

Preparation Time: 30 Minutes
Cooking Time: 55 minutes
Servings: 3
Ingredients:

- 8 eggs
- Pinch cinnamon and cloves
- 2 garlic cloves
- 1 teaspoon nutmeg
- 2 tablespoons chopped parsley
- 1 tablespoon chives
- 1 teaspoon tarragon leaves
- 2 ½ teaspoons salt
- 1 teaspoon pepper
- 1kg ground pork

Directions:

1. Pre-heat an oven over medium heat, cover the baking tray with the parchment.
2. Heat a pan over high heat, pour water and bring to a boil. Add eggs, boil them for about 10 to 15 minutes. Peel them off. Apart from, mince garlic cloves, add parsley, salt, chives, nutmeg, pepper, tarragon leaves, cinnamon and cloves. Add spice mixture to the ground pork, combine well with your hands. Divide the mixture into 8 parts and wrap them around the peeled eggs and transfer the balls to the baking tray.

3. Finally bake for about 20 to 25 minutes over medium heat, increase the heat to medium-high and bake for about 5 to 8 more minutes.

15. Funny Sautéed Kale

Preparation Time: 15 to 20 Minutes
Cooking Time: 15 to 20 Minutes
Servings: 2 to 3
Ingredients:

- 2 tablespoons sliced almonds

- A pinch of sea salt to taste
- 1/4 onion (Diced)
- 1 ½ tablespoon extra-virgin olive oil
- 2 garlic cloves (Minced)
- 4 cups rinsed and chopped kale

Directions:

1. First of all, quickly heat extra virgin olive oil in a medium skillet set over medium heat; add onion and saute for about 5 to 10 minutes or until translucent.
2. Add garlic, kale and almonds and cook properly for about 5 to 10 minutes or until kale is tender. Finally season with sea salt to serve.

16. Reliable Blueberry and Dates- Breakfast cereal

Preparation Time: 20 to 30 Minutes
Cooking Time: 30 to 40 Minutes
Servings: 4 to 6
Ingredients:

- ½ cup unsweetened coconut flakes
- 1 tsp. sea salt
- 1 cup pumpkin seeds

- 1 tablespoon vanilla
- 2 cups almond flour
- 2 ½ teaspoons Cinnamon
- 6 medium dates, pitted
- 1/3 cup coconut oil
- ½ cup dried blueberries

Directions:

1. Preheat your oven to about 310 to 320°F.
2. Add coconut oil, dates and half the almond flour to a food processor and mix it thoroughly. Add pumpkin seeds and continue pulsing until roughly chopped. Next, transfer the mixture to a large bowl and add cinnamon, vanilla and salt; spread on a baking sheet and bake for about 20 to 25 minutes or until browned.
3. Finally remove from the oven and let cool slightly before stirring in blueberries and coconut.

17. Charming Lemon Thyme Lamb Chops

Preparation Time: 20 to 25 minutes
Cooking Time: 10 to 15 minutes
Servings: 2 to 4
Ingredients:

- Sea salt

- Lemon juice – 1
- Olive oil about 1/4 cup
- Fresh thyme
- Lamb chops – 4

Directions:

1. In a large dish, place the lamb chops then cover with lemon juice, oil and thyme leaves.
2. Cover the mixture and let sit at room temperature for about 20 minutes. Turn the chops to

marinate evenly. Apart from, preheated a pan; lower the heat and grill the chops for about 2 to 5 minutes per side. Grill the lemons with the chops. Finally serve immediately then sprinkle with fresh thyme leaves and sea salt.

18. Energetic Baked Salmon with Lemon and Thyme

Preparation Time: 10 minutes
Cooking Time: 25 minutes
Servings: 4 to 6
Ingredients:

- About 1.5 lemon, sliced thin
- Olive oil, for drizzling
- About 1.5 tbsp. capers
- 1 tbsp. fresh thyme
- Salt and freshly ground pepper
- 32 oozes piece of salmon

Directions:

1. Line a rimmed baking sheet with parchment paper and then place salmon, skin side down, on the prepared baking sheet; then generously season salmon with salt and pepper. Arrange capers on the salmon, and top with sliced lemon and thyme. Place baking sheet in a cold oven, then turn heat to 400° F.

2. Finally bake for about 20 to 25 minutes. Serve immediately.

19. Dashing Garlic Mushrooms

Preparation Time: 15 minutes
Cooking Time: 5 hours
Servings: 6
Ingredients:

- 4 garlic cloves (Minced)
- 2 ½ tablespoons parsley (Chopped)
- 24 ounces mushroom caps
- 2 tablespoons olive oil
- ¼ teaspoon thyme dried
- Black pepper to the taste
- 1 teaspoon basil (Dried)
- ½ teaspoon oregano (Dried)
- 2 bay leaves
- 1 cup veggie stock

Directions:

1. Grease your slow cooker with the olive oil. Add mushrooms, basil, bay leaves, thyme, oregano, garlic, black pepper and stock, then cover and cook properly on low for about 3 to 4 hours. Stir frequently. Finally divide between plates and serve with parsley sprinkled on top.

20. Scrumptious Crispy Sea Bass

Preparation Time: 20 Minutes
Cooking Time: 6 hours
Servings: 6
Ingredients:

- 3 filets of sea bass, skin on
- Juice of ½ a lemon
- Salt and pepper to taste
- 1/4 teaspoon red pepper flakes
- 4 ½ tablespoons ghee or coconut oil, divided

Directions:

1. Put 3 tablespoons of ghee or coconut oil to a heavy bottomed skillet. Heat it over medium-high heat. Meanwhile, sprinkle the filets with salt, pepper and red pepper flakes on both sides.

2. Before placing the fish into the skillet, carefully drag, skin side down, it across the skillet back and forth couple times, lifting it up each time to heat the fish skin and avoid the fish from getting stuck to the bottom. Then cook the fillets for about 5 to 10 minutes, until the skin is crispy, then turn the filets and add the rest of ghee or oil and few squeezes of lemon.

3. Cook properly for about 5 to 10 more minutes, basting the fish once in a while.

4. When it is cooked through and opaque in color, remove it and place on a serving plate. Sprinkle with sea salt and drizzle with lemon juice (optional). Finally serve with veggies or other side dishes.

21. Nostalgic Chipotle Beef Lettuce Wraps

Preparation Time: 15 Minutes
Cooking Time: 20 minutes
Servings: 6
Ingredients:

- 1 ½ tablespoon coconut oil
- Salt, pepper, and lime to taste
- ½ cup organic tomato paste
- Any vegetables you wish
- 1 finely diced red onion
- 1 ½ tablespoon chopped jalapeno
- Lettuce leaves
- Pinch of dried chili flakes
- 1/2-pound ground beef
- ½ teaspoon cumin

Directions:

1. Heat coconut oil in a saucepan and cook properly the ground beef until browned. Drain and set aside. In that same pan, add the red onion and sauté until soft.

2. Next, add jalapenos, vegetables of choice, cumin, dried chili flakes, and tomato sauce; then stir until it thickens around the edges of the pan.

3. Add beef into the mixture and let it sit for about 5 to 10 minutes, stirring occasionally.

4. Finally add mixture to the lettuce leaves, spritz with lime juice or salt and pepper, and enjoy!

22. Best Paleo Crock Pot Beef Chili

Preparation Time: 15 minutes
Cooking Time: 4 to 6 hours
Servings: 4 to 6
Ingredients:

- 4 garlic cloves (Minced)
- Salt and pepper to taste
- 1 medium onion (Diced)
- ½ teaspoon cayenne
- 1 green pepper (Diced)
- 1 ½ red pepper (Diced)
- ½ tablespoon cumin
- 1 tomato (Diced)
- 2 pounds lean ground beef
- 3 celery stalks (Diced)
- 1/4 cup green chilies (Diced)
- 28 ounces jar crushed tomatoes
- 1 tablespoon oregano
- 2 tablespoons chili powder
- 15 ounces can tomato sauce
- ½ tablespoon basil

Directions:

1. Put all the ingredients to your pot, or crock pot if you have. Stir until combined.

2. Cover and cook properly on low for about 5 to 6 hours.
3. Serve in bowls and garnish with cilantro. Finally, side with tortilla chips.

23. Vintage Carrot and orange cake

Preparation Time: 20 minutes

Cooking Time: 90 minutes
Servings: 1 to 2 cake
Ingredients:
- 2 large carrots
- 3 cups almond flour
- About 6.5 tablespoons honey raw
- Juice of half the orange
- Zest of 1 orange
- 6 eggs

Directions:
1. Preheat oven to 320 °F.
2. Cut the carrots into 1-inch pieces, put them in a boiling water and cook properly until fork-tender. Separate whites and yolks.
3. Drain the carrots and blend the, in a food processor. Then combine carrots with almond flour, orange zest and juice. Beat the yolks with honey and add to the mixture, then beat the white to soft peaks and carefully add them too. Rub a spring cake tin with butter and pour in the mixture. Bake for about 50 to 55 minutes, until a toothpick inserted in the middle comes out clean. Next, cool for about 15 to 18 minutes before opening the tin. Finally serve warm, cut into pieces.

24. Lucky Berry omelet

Preparation Time: 20 minutes
Cooking Time: 20 minutes
Servings: 2 to 3
Ingredients:
- 50g blueberries
- Bunch mint leaves
- About 55g blackberries
- 2 tablespoons coconut oil
- 50g raspberries
- 4 eggs

Directions:
1. Pre-heat a frying pan over medium heat, pour 1 tablespoon coconut oil.
2. Whisk eggs in the bowl, transfer half of them to the pan. Cook properly for about 2 to 5 minutes. Add half of the berries and fold the omelet to cover the berries and cook properly for about 2 more minute. Finally remove to a plate and repeat the process with the remaining ingredients.

Paleo Lunch Recipes

25. Chicken Broth

Preparation Time: 6 hours
Cooking Time: 6 hours
Servings: 6
Ingredients:

- 4 lbs. fresh whole chicken
- 2 peeled onions
- 2 celery stalks
- 1 carrot
- 8 black peppercorns
- 2 sprigs fresh thyme
- 2 sprigs fresh parsley
- 1 teaspoon salt

Directions:

Put all ingredients in your pot and cook on low for 6 hours. Let cool to warm room temperature and strain. Keep chilled and use or freeze broth within a few days.

26. Lentil Soup

Preparation Time: 4 hours
Cooking Time: 4 hours
Servings: 6
Ingredients

- 2 tablespoons olive oil
- 1 cup chopped onion
- ½ chopped carrot
- ½ chopped celery
- 2 teaspoons salt
- pound lentils
- 3 chopped tomatoes
- 2 cups vegetable broth
- ½ teaspoon coriander
- ½ teaspoon cumin

Instructions

Put all ingredients in the slow cooker and cook on low for 4 hours.

27. Spicy Turkey Chili

Cooking Time: 15 minutes
Preparation Time: 3 hours 45 minutes
Servings: 6
Ingredients:

- 2 pounds boneless, cutted turkey thighs
- 1 yellow onion
- 3 chopped garlic cloves
- 2 jalapeno pepper, seeded
- 2 tablespoons chili powder
- 1 can chiles
- 2 larghe tomatoes
- 15 ounces black beans, drained
- 1 tablespoon white vinegar
- Salt and pepper to taste
- Minced cilantro for serving

Directions:

1. Fill a pot with 3/4 of water. Add in chopped turkey, chopped onion, garlic, chopped jalapeño, chopped tomatoes, chili powder. Season with salt and pepper. Cover with the lid and cook on medium for 3 hours. Add beans and cook for another 30 minutes, then stir in vinegar and cook for another 10 minutes. Serve with sliced cilantro.

28. Iconic Simple Zucchini Fritters

Preparation Time: 10 minutes
Cooking Time: 25 minutes
Servings: 2
Ingredients:

- Sea salt and pepper to taste
- Coconut oil or ghee for cooking
- 1/4 cup coconut flour
- ½ teaspoon cayenne pepper
- 1 egg, beaten
- 2 medium zucchinis, shredded

Directions:

1. Use a grater or a food processor with a shredding blade, quickly shred the zucchini.
2. Add salt to the shredded zucchini and mix.
3. Please set aside for about 10 to 15 minutes and then quickly rinse under water to remove the salt. Remove all the moisture from the zucchini as much as possible so that they won't be soggy; then mix in coconut flour egg, black pepper and cayenne pepper. Add oil to a large skillet and melt it over medium-low heat.
4. Make patties from the zucchini mixture, about 1/4 cup for each one, and add to the skillet.
5. Cook in batches until browned, about 2 to 5 minutes. Add more oil as needed.
6. Finally let them fritters cool on a cooling rack before serving.

29. Awesome Asian Stir Fry with Bacon

Preparation Time: 10 minutes
Cooking Time: 15 minutes
Servings: 2
Ingredients:

- 3 slices of bacon
- Tamari sauce to taste
- 3 ½ tablespoons coconut oil
- Salt to taste
- 2 ½ tablespoons chopped cilantro
- 12 oozes chopped Asian stir fry package

Directions:

1. Place the coconut oil or ghee in a saucepan and heat over medium heat until melted.
2. Place vegetables into pan and saute until soft, which is about 10 to 15 minutes.
3. While the vegetables are cooking, reheat or cook the bacon in a separate pan (or in the microwave, whichever you have chosen to cook with)
4. Finally, once vegetables are soft, add the cilantro, salt, and tamari sauce to taste. Enjoy!

30. Super Paleo Mexican Beef Stew

Preparation Time: 25 minutes
Cooking Time: 6 hours 5 minutes
Servings: 2
Ingredients:

- 1 garlic clove (Minced)
- Pinch of salt and fresh ground pepper
- About 1 red onion (Chopped)
- 2 cups of water
- 4 ounces green chilies (Diced)
- 3 large tomatoes (Chopped)
- 1 teaspoon cumin
- About 1.5 teaspoon oregano
- 2 teaspoons chili powder
- 1-pound stewing beef

- 2 cups beef broth

Directions:

1. Slice the stewing beef into thin slices. Place all the ingredients in your pot.
2. Cover and cook properly on low for about 4 to 5 hours. Finally serve in bowls.

31. Beef Broth

Cooking Time: 6 hours 45 minutes
Preparation Time: 6 hour 45 minutes
Servings: 4
Ingredients:

- 5 pounds beef meets
- 1 pound of stew meat cutted
- Olive oil
- 1-2 onions, chopped
- 2 large carrots, chopped
- 1 celery rib, chopped
- 2 cloves of garlic
- Handful of parsley
- 1-2 bay leaves
- 10 peppercorns

Directions:

1. Heat oven to 375°F. Rub olive oil over the stew meat pieces, carrots, and onions. Place stew meat or beef scraps, stock bones, carrots and onions in a large roasting pan. Roast in oven for about 45 minutes, turning everything half-way through the cooking. Place everything from the oven in the slow cooker and cook on low for 6 hours. After cooking, remove the bones and vegetables from the pot. Strain the broth. Let cool to room temperature and then put in the refrigerator. The fat will solidify once the broth has chilled. Discard the fat (or reuse it) and pour the broth into a jar and freeze it.

32. Black Bean Soup

Cooking Time: 8 hours
Servings: 6
Ingredients

- 14 tablespoons cup oil
- 1/2 Onion, Diced
- 1/4 cup Carrots, Diced
- 1/2 Green Bell Pepper, Diced
- 1 cup beef broth
- 2 pounds raw Black Beans
- 1 tablespoon lemon juice
- 1/2 Garlic clove
- Salt and pepper to taste
- 2 teaspoons Chili Powder
- 8-pounds pork meat
- 1 tablespoon flour
- 1/2 cup water

Instructions

Put all ingredients in slow cooker and cook on low for 8 hours.

33. Squash soup

Servings: 6
Cooking Time: 4 hours
Ingredients

- 1 Squash, seeds removed, chopped
- 1 carrot, chopped
- 1 onion (diced)
- 1 cup coconut milk
- 1/2 cup water

- 2 tablespoons Olive oil
- Salt and pepper to taste

- 2 teaspoons cinnamon
- 2 teaspoons turmeric

Instructions

Put all ingredients in the slow cooker and cook on low for 4 hours. Blend until smooth and creamy. Sprinkle it with toasted pumpkin seeds.

34. Happy Chicken, Leek and Asparagus Dill Casserole

Preparation Time: 15 Minutes
Cooking Time: 45 Minutes
Servings: 2
Ingredients:
- 250g Minced Chicken
- Sea salt and pepper
- 1/4 cup coconut milk

- ½ tsp. garlic powder
- 4 free range eggs, beaten
- 1 thinly sliced leek
- ½ tbsp. minced fresh dill
- 4 stalks asparagus, chopped
- Coconut oil, for greasing

Directions:

1. Preheat your oven to 320°F. Grease a square baking dish and set aside.
2. Place the chicken mince in a pan set over medium heat; break them into small pieces.
3. Cook for a few minutes and add asparagus and leeks; continue cooking for about 5 to 8 minutes more or maybe until chicken is no longer pink. Next, remove the pan from heat, discarding excess fat.
4. Finally whisk together eggs, coconut milk, garlic powder, dill, salt and pepper in a bowl; pour the mixture into the prepared baking dish and then quickly add the chicken mixture; mix well and then bake for about 45 to 48 minutes or maybe until set in the center.

35. Lucky Curried Chicken Salad

Preparation Time: 15 minutes
Cooking Time: 2 hours
Servings: 4
Ingredients:
- Cubed cooked chicken – 1 pound
- Fresh chives (Optional)
- Chopped jicama – 1/2 cup
- Small papayas, peeled and sliced in half
- Thinly sliced celery – 1 cup
- Mayonnaise – 1/4 cup
- Red curry paste – about 1.5 teaspoon
- Lemon flavor yogurt – 1/4 cup
- Soy sauce – about 2.5 teaspoons
- Orange – 1

Directions:

1. Peel orange, then segment into half or quarter. Place chicken, orange, grapes, jicama and celery in a bowl and combine.
2. For dressing use a small mixing bowl to combine mayonnaise, soy sauce, yogurt, and curry paste together.
3. Pour the dressing over the chicken mixture then toss lightly so as to coat. Cover the mixture and allow to chill for a period of 1 hour or more. Finally serve in papaya halves or garnish with fresh chives.

36. Veggie Minestrone

Servings: 8
Cooking Time: 4 hours
Preparation Time: 4 hours 30 minutes
Ingredients

- 3 tablespoons olive oil
- 3 garlic cloves, chopped
- 1 onion, chopped
- 2 cups chopped celery
- 4 carrots, sliced
- 2 cups chicken broth
- 2 cups water
- 3 cups tomato sauce
- 1/2 cup red wine
- 1 cup raw kidney beans
- 1 cups green beans
- 2 cups baby spinach, rinsed
- 2 zucchinis, quartered and sliced
- 1 tablespoon chopped oregano
- 2 tablespoons chopped basil
- Salt and pepper to taste

Instructions

Put all ingredients in the slow cooker and cook on low for 4 hours.

37. Vegetarian Chili

Servings: 6
Cooking Time: 5 hours
Ingredients

- 1 tablespoon olive oil
- 1 cup chopped onions
- ½ cup chopped carrots
- 2 garlic cloves, minced
- ½ chopped green bell pepper
- ½ chopped red bell pepper
- ½ cup chopped celery
- 1 tablespoons chili powder
- 1 cup chopped mushrooms
- 3 cups chopped tomatoes
- 2 cups raw kidney beans
- 1 tablespoons ground cumin
- ½ teaspoon oregano
- ½ teaspoon minced basil leaves

Instructions

Put all ingredients in the slow cooker and cook on low for 5 hours.

38. Braised Green Peas with Beef

Servings: 4
Cooking Time: 4 hours

Ingredients

- 2 cups fresh green peas

- 2 onions, finely chopped
- 2 garlic cloves chopped
- 1/2 chopped fresh ginger
- 1/2 teaspoon red pepper flakes
- 1 tomato, roughly chopped
- 2 chopped carrots
- 2 tablespoons olive oil
- 2 cups chicken broth
- 1-pound cubed beef
- Salt and pepper to taste

Directions:

Put all ingredients in the slow cooker and cook on low for 4 hours.

39. White Chicken Chili

Servings: 4

Cooking Time: 4 hours

Ingredients

- 4 large boneless chicken breasts
- 2 green bell peppers
- 1 large onion
- 2 jalapenos
- 1/2 cup diced green chilies
- 1/2 cup white onions
- 2 tablespoons olive oil
- 3 cups cooked white beans
- 3 cups vegetable broth
- 1 teaspoon cumin
- Salt and pepper to taste

Instructions

Put all ingredients in the slow cooker and cook on low for 4 hours.

40. Kale White Bean Pork Soup

Servings: 6   **Cooking Time:** 8 hours   **Ingredients:**

- 2 tablespoons olive oil
- 3 tablespoons chili powder
- 1 tablespoon jalapeno hot sauce
- 2 pounds bone-in pork chops
- Salt
- 4 stalks celery, chopped
- 1 large white onion, chopped
- 3 cloves garlic, chopped
- 2 cups chicken broth
- 2 cups diced tomatoes
- 2 cups raw white beans
- 6 cups packed Kale

Instructions

Put all ingredients in the slow cooker and cook for 8 hours on low.

41. Greek lemon chicken soup

Servings: 4

Cooking Time: 4 hours

Ingredients:

- 4 cups chicken broth
- 1/4 cup uncooked brown rice
- Salt and pepper to taste
- 3 eggs
- 3 tablespoons lemon juice
- Handful fresh dill (chopped)
- Shredded roasted chicken

Directions:

1. In a bowl whisk lemon juice and the eggs until smooth. Add about 1 cup of the hot broth into the egg/lemon mixture and whisk to combine.
2. Put all ingredients in the slow cooker and cook on low for 4 hours.

42. Fantastic Nori salmon handroll

Preparation Time: 10 minutes
Cooking Time: 15 minutes
Servings: 3
Ingredients:

- 1 green onion
- 1 toasted nori sheet
- 2 cucumbers
- 1/4 avocado
- 2 ½ ounces wild canned salmon

Directions:

1. First of all, slice avocado and cucumber and finely chop green onion.
2. Next, put the nori paper on a cutting board, layer the avocado, fish, 2 slices of cucumber and green onion. Finally wrap the paper around. Serve.

43. Great Amazing Eggplant Dip

Preparation Time: 15 minutes
Cooking Time: 4 hours and 10 to 15 minutes
Servings: 6
Ingredients:

- 1 zucchini (Chopped)
- Salt and pepper to taste
- 2 ½ tablespoons olive oil
- 2 tablespoons balsamic vinegar
- 1 ½ teaspoons garlic, minced
- 1 tablespoon parsley, chopped
- 1 yellow onion, chopped
- 3 tablespoons tomato paste
- 1 celery stick, chopped
- 1 tomato, chopped
- 1 eggplant

Directions:

1. First of all, brush eggplant with half of the oil, place them on a pan and cook properly over medium high heat for about 5 to 8 minutes on each side. Then quickly leave aside to cool down and then chop it. Grease your slow cooker with the rest of the oil and add eggplant pieces.
2. Add, onion, zucchini, vinegar, parsley, celery, tomato, tomato paste, salt and garlic, pepper and stir everything. Cover and cook properly on low heat for about 3 to 4 hours. Stir frequently.
3. Finally stir your spread again very well, divide into bowls and serve.

44. Kale Pork

Servings: 4
Cooking Time: 4 hours
Ingredients

- 2 tablespoons olive oil
- 1-pound pork meat, cutted
- 2 teaspoons salt
- 1 onion, chopped
- 4 garlic cloves, minced
- 2 teaspoons paprika
- 1/2 red pepper

- 1 cup white wine
- 4 tomatoes, chopped
- 4 cups chicken broth
- 1 bunch kale, chopped
- 2 cups cooked white beans

Instructions

Put all ingredients in the slow cooker and cook on low for 4 hours.

45. Barbecued Beef

Servings: 8

Ingredients

Cooking Time: 4 hours

- ½ cups tomato paste
- 2 tablespoons lemon juice
- 2 tablespoons mustard
- Salt and pepper to taste
- ½ garlic clove
- 4 pounds boneless chuck roast

Instructions

Place chuck roast in a slow cooker. Pour all ingredients over and mix well. Cover, and cook on low for 4 hours.

46. Superfoods Chili

Servings: 6   **Cooking Time:** 4 hours   **Ingredients**

- 2 tablespoons olive oil
- 2 onions, chopped
- 3 garlic cloves, minced
- pound ground beef
- 2 cups beef sirloin, cubed
- 2 cups diced tomatoes
- 1 cup strong brewed coffee
- 1 cup tomato paste
- 2 cups beef broth
- 1 tablespoons cumin seeds
- 1 tablespoon cocoa powder
- 1 teaspoon ground coriander
- Salt and pepper to taste
- 6 cups cooked kidney beans
- 4 fresh hot chili peppers, chopped

Instructions

Put all ingredients in the slow cooker and cook on low for 4 hours.

47. Best Cuban Picadillo

Preparation Time: 15 minutes

Cooking Time: 25 minutes

Servings: 2

Ingredients:

- Garlic – 2 cloves, minced
- Alcaparrado or green olives – 2 tbsp.
- Chopped tomato – 1
- Pepper – 1/2, finely chopped
- Bay leaf – 1 or 2
- Cilantro – about 2.5 tbsp.
- Lean ground beef – 1 -1/2 lb. 93%
- Ground cumin – 1 tsp.
- Tomato sauce – 1/2 can (4 oz.)
- Kosher salt
- Onion – about 1 chopped large
- Fresh ground pepper

Directions:

1. In a large pan, brown meat on high heat. Break up the meat into smaller pieces and season with salt and pepper. Drain all juice from pan, when meat is no longer pink.
2. Meanwhile, chop cilantro, pepper, tomato, garlic and onion. Add them to the meat and continue to cook on low heat. Add Alcaparrado, bay leaf, cumin and more salt according to taste. Add 1/4 cup of water and tomato sauce and mix well.
3. Finally, lower heat and simmer 20 to 25 minutes, covered.

48. Grain Free Balls with Sauce

Preparation Time: 10 minutes
Cooking Time: 30 minutes
Servings: 4
Ingredients:

- 1 pound of grass-fed ground beef
- 5 tablespoons of sweet grape jelly
- ½ a cup of organic chili sauce
- ½ a teaspoon ground pepper
- 1 teaspoon of ground garlic salt
- ½ a teaspoon of chili powder
- ½ a teaspoon of paprika
- 1 piece of egg
- ¼ cup of arrowroot

Directions:

1. Take a bowl and add beef, garlic, pepper, salt, egg and arrowroot.
2. Make nice golf balls and assemble them in your pot.
3. Add jelly, chili sauce, chili powder and paprika to the bottom of your pot.
4. Cook them on low heat for about 30 minutes. Once done, serve!

49. Korea's Innocent Short Ribs

Preparation Time: 10 minutes
Cooking Time: 45 minutes
Servings: 4
Ingredients:

- 5 pounds of bone-in short ribs
- Salt and pepper to taste
- ½ a cup of coconut aminos
- 1 tablespoon of rice vinegar
- 2 teaspoons of Red Boat Fish Sauce
- 1 medium sized Asian Pear
- 6 peeled and chopped garlic cloves
- 3 chopped scallions
- 1 fresh ginger cut up into 2-inch pieces
- Small handful of chopped cilantro

Directions:

1. Pat the ribs dry using a paper towel and season it with pepper and salt. Rub it all over.
2. Transfer your seasoned ribs to your pot.
3. Meanwhile, add the coconut aminos, fish sauce, vinegar, pear, scallions, garlic and ginger to a blender. Mix them properly. Pour the sauce over your ribs in the pot and stir properly.
4. Cover and cook it for about 45 minutes on high, turning them at half cooking.
5. Turn off the heat, but don't remove the lid to release heat naturally.
6. Check if they are soft enough to be picked by a fork, if not then cook for another 5-10 minutes.

7. Transfer the ribs to your platter and season the liquid. Skim the fat and scoop the sauce on top of your ribs. Garnish it with a bit of cilantro and serve!

50. Mediterranean Turkey Sandwich

Preparation Time: 10 minutes
Cooking Time: 10 minutes
Servings: 1
Ingredients:

- Sprouted grain– 2 slices
- Smoked turkey – 2 slices
- Spinach – 1/3 cup
- Hummus – 2 tablespoons
- Sliced avocado – ½
- Red onion – 4 rings
- Sliced apple – 1/2

Directions:

1. Put the bread slices on a cutting board or a flat plate and spread hummus on them.
2. Prepare the turkey by layering it with the sliced avocado, spinach, sliced apple and red onion rings. Cut this preparation in half and enjoy!

51. Delicious Goulash

Servings: 6
Cooking Time: 4 hours
Ingredients

- 3 cups cauliflower
- 2 pounds ground beef
- 1 red onion, chopped
- Salt and pepper to taste
- 1 garlic clove
- 2 cups cooked kidney beans
- 1 cup tomato paste

Directions:

Put all ingredients in the slow cooker and cook on low for 4 hours.

52. Cabbage Stewed with Meat

Servings: 8
Cooking Time: 4 hours
Ingredients

- 2 pounds ground beef
- 1 cup beef stock
- 1 chopped red onion
- 1 bay leaf
- salt and pepper to taste
- 2 sliced celery ribs
- 4 cups shredded cabbage
- 1 carrot, sliced
- 1 cup tomato paste

Instructions

Put all ingredients in the slow cooker and cook on low for 4 hours.

53. Beef Stew with Peas and Carrots

Servings: 8
Cooking Time: 6 hours
Ingredients

- 3 large chopped carrots
- 1 large chopped onion
- 2 tablespoons olive oil
- 1 garlic clove minced
- 2 cups green peas

- 4 cups beef stock
- Salt and pepper to taste
- 4 pounds boneless chuck roast

Instructions

Put all ingredients in the slow cooker and cook on low for 6 hours.

54. Vintage Coconut Chicken w/ Mustard- Honey Sauce

Preparation Time: 20 to 25 Minutes
Cooking Time: 15 to 20 Minutes
Servings: 2 to 3
Ingredients:

- 1 cup unsweetened coconut flakes
- 1 cup steamed vegetables for serving
- 2 free range eggs
- 1/2 cup honey
- About 1 cup coconut flour
- 1/2 cup Dijon mustard
- 2 pounds boneless chicken breasts

Directions:

1. Preheat your oven to 400°F and line baking sheet with parchment paper. Then rinse the chicken and slice into small strips; pat them dry and set aside. Place coconut flour onto a plate and set aside. In a bowl, whisk the eggs and set aside. Place coconut flakes in another plate and set aside. Dip the chicken strips into the coconut flour, then into the eggs and finally into coconut flakes; arrange them onto the prepared baking sheet and bake for about 15 to 20 minutes or until browned. Finally, meanwhile, combine honey and mustard in a bowl; drizzle over the baked chicken strips and serve with steamed veggies.

55. Beef Meatballs with White Beans

Servings: 8
Cooking Time: 2 hours 20 minutes
Ingredients

- 2 pounds beef meat
- 2 tablespoons olive oil
- 1 sprig thyme, minced
- 2 cups uncooked white navy beans
- 4 cups beef stock
- Salt and pepper to taste
- 1 chopped onion
- 1 bunch chopped parsley
- 1 cup chopped carrots

Instructions

1. Take a pot and add 4 cups beef stock, salt, pepper, withe beans and beef meat and cook on low for 2 hours more. Turn off the heat.

2. Take a food processor and mix the beef meat mixture, thyme, chopped onion, parsley, and chopped carrots. Blend until uniform. Make 16 meatballs. Add them to the bot from before and cook for 20 minutes on low. Garnish with parsley and serve!

Very Healthy Recipes for Dinner

56. Tasty Paleo Delicious Zucchini Smoothie

Preparation Time: 5 to 10 Minutes

Cooking Time: 15 minutes

Servings: 2 to 4

Ingredients:

- 1 Brown Onion
- 2 Cups of water
- 2.5 tbsps. Coconut Oil
- 1 Large Zucchini

Directions:

1. First of all, rinse and pat dry and cut the Zucchini into slices. Chop the onion.
2. Heat the coconut oil in a pan under moderate heat and fry the onions until golden brown.
3. Add the Zucchini and cook properly under medium heat until tender.
4. Add 2 cups of water and boil. When boiling blend together.
5. Finally add a dash of salt to taste. Enjoy!

57. Yummy Kale Omelets

Preparation Time: 2 to 5 minutes

Cooking Time: 5 to 10 minutes

Servings: 1 to 3

Ingredients:

- Salt and pepper
- Chopped kale – 1 cup
- ½ tablespoon chopped chives
- Eggs – 3
- Butter – 1 tablespoon

Directions:

1. First of all, place a frying pan over medium heat then add butter and heat.
2. Add kale to the pan then cook properly for about 5 to 10 minutes or until soft.
3. Beat the eggs in a bowl then add fresh chives, pepper and salt.
4. Add egg mixture to the frying pan then swirl the pan for the mixture to spread to the edges.
5. Cook properly on low heat until well set at the top. Finally fold over and serve.

58. Turkey Handmade Sausage

Preparation Time: 10 Minutes

Cooking Time: 25 minutes

Servings: 2 to 4

Ingredients:

- Olive oil – about 1.5 tsp.
- Pinch raw sugar
- Onion – 1 small, diced small
- Pinch nutmeg
- Garlic – 1 large clove, chopped
- Kosher salt and black pepper to taste
- Fennel seed – about 1.5 tsp.
- Paprika – 3/4 tsp.
- Lean ground turkey – 1 lb. 93%
- Red wine vinegar – 1 tbsp.
- Cooking spray

- Chopped chives – 1 tbsp.

Directions:

1. Over medium-low heat, heat a medium skillet. Add oil, garlic and onion.
2. Stir and then cook until onion is translucent about 8 to 10 minutes. If needed, lower the heat.
3. Add fennel and cook properly for about 2 minutes or until fragrant and toasted.
4. Place the mixture in a medium bowl, then add sugar, chives, nutmeg, paprika, red wine vinegar and ground turkey to the bowl with onion-fennel mixture. Mix well with a fork.
5. Make 6 even patties and place on a parchment paper. Spray a skillet with cooking spray and place over medium-low heat. Brown turkey patties in the hot pan in 2 batches.
6. Cook 3 minutes on each side. Once the patties get a browned crust on each side; lower the heat and cover. Continue to cook properly until the internal temperature reaches 150 to 160°F.
7. Finally, remove and cook the second batch.

59. Tomatoes and Avocado Omelet

Preparation Time: 5 minutes   **Cooking Time:** 10 minutes   **Servings:** 2

Ingredients:

- 1 tablespoon olive oil
- ½ fresh avocado sliced into
- 1 green onions (Diced)
- 2 small tomatoes
- 1 cup fresh spinach leaves
- 2 eggs, scrambled

Directions:

1. Heat olive oil on low in nonstick omelet pan. Saute onions until tender. Add eggs and cook properly on low for about 2 to 5 minutes.

2. Add remaining ingredients, chopped. Finally, fold and flip omelet until eggs are fully cooked.

60. Legendary Omelet with Avocado and Pico De Gallo

Preparation Time: 15 minutes

Cooking Time: 10 minutes

Servings: 1 to 2

Ingredients:

- Pico de Gallo – about 2.5 tablespoons
- Egg – 1 large

- Egg white – 1 large
- Avocado – 1 ounce (Sliced)
- Salt and pepper to taste
- Cooking spray

Directions:

1. In a small or maybe medium bowl, beat the egg white and egg; then season with salt and pepper.
2. Heat a nonstick skillet over medium heat and then spray oil-cooking spray. Pour the eggs and cook properly for about 2 to 5 minutes, or until set. Transfer to a plate.
3. Finally, top with Pico de Gallo and avocado and enjoy.

61. Quick Eggs Benedict on Artichoke Hearts

Preparation Time: 20 minutes   **Servings:** 1 to 2

Cooking Time: 1 hours 10 minutes   **Ingredients:**

- Salt and pepper to taste
- As much turkey breasts, chopped
- ½ cup balsamic vinegar
- 2 cups artichoke hearts
- 2 eggs
- Hollandaise sauce
- 1 cup melted ghee
- 3 egg yolks
- Pinch of paprika
- 3/4 tablespoon lemon juice
- Pinch of salt
- 1 egg white

Directions:

1. Line baking sheet with foil and preheat oven to 370° F.
2. Remove artichoke hearts from their dressing and place them in the balsamic vinegar for at least 15 to 20 minutes (but do not go over 30).
3. Fill a pot of water and simmer it on your stove for the Hollandaise sauce. Melt the ghee (or butter) in a separate saucepan. Separate your eggs, placing the yolks in a cooking bowl and hang on to the egg whites. Take the artichoke hearts out of the marinade and then place them on the foil-lined sheet. Brush them with the egg white before placing the turkey breasts over the artichokes' tops in a layer-like fashion. Put the tray in the oven for about 20 to 28 minutes.
4. Whisk the egg yolks in the lemon juice, then place the bowl (preferably stainless steel) over the pot of simmering water. This should create a double boiler. Then, slowly add the ghee (or butter) and a little bit of salt. Whisk it until it doubles in size and looks silky, then set aside. Turn up the heat on the pot of water and get it boiling.
5. Crack the eggs in one at a time into a ladle, and then slide that spoon full of egg into the water. This will poach the eggs that go on top of the turkey breasts.
6. Let them sit in the water for 2 minutes, and then remove.
7. Take out the artichoke hearts and turkey breasts (if not already out) and lay them on a plate.
8. Finally place the poached egg on top and pour the Hollandaise sauce on top.
9. Sprinkle with salt, pepper, and paprika to taste. Enjoy!

62. Wonderful Paleo Crock Pot Chicken Soup

Preparation Time: 40 minutes   **Cooking Time:** 6 hours 10 minutes   **Servings:** 5

Ingredients:

- 4 cups filtered water
- 3 carrots, diced
- 3 celery stalks, diced
- Salt and pepper
- 1 tablespoon herbs de Provence
- 2 chicken thighs, with bone
- 2 chicken breasts, with bone, with skin
- 1 ½ teaspoon apple cider vinegar
- 1 medium onion, diced

Directions:

1. Place all the ingredients in a pot (or in a crock pot, if you have), ensuring the chicken is placed on top of the vegetables, bone should be side down. Add 4 cups of water, to cover the ingredients.

Cook properly on low for about 5 to 6 hours, until meat flakes off bone and vegetables are fork tender. Once cooked, take out the chicken. Remove skin and bones.

2. Shred the chicken with 2 forks. Return pieces to the soup. Stir well. Taste. Season if needed.

3. Finally serve in bowls.

63. Iconic Italian Pulled Pork Ragu

Preparation Time: 5 Minutes
Cooking Time: 30 minutes
Servings: 2 to 4
Ingredients:

- 2 tablespoons minced parsley, divided
- Salt and pepper, to taste
- 2 bay leaves
- 1 teaspoon olive oil
- 4 garlic cloves, smashed with knife
- 2 sprigs fresh thyme
- 4 cups of finely chopped tomatoes
- 7 ounce roasted red peppers, drained
- 18 ounces pork tenderloin

Directions:

1. First of all, sprinkle the pork tenderloin with salt and pepper. Smash garlic cloves with the side of a knife. Finely chop tomatoes. Add oil to a preheated large pot.

2. Add garlic and sauté over medium-high heat for about 2 minutes, until golden; then remove the garlic with a slotted spoon and set aside. Add pork and brown it on each side for about 2 to 5 minutes. Add tomatoes, fresh thyme, red peppers, bay leave and half of the chopped parsley.

3. Bring to a boil, cover, and cook properly on low heat for about 2.5 hours, until the fork is fork tender. Remove bay leaves and then shred the pork with 2 forks; serve over pasta topped with the remaining parsley.

64. Super Paleo One Pot Fajita Soup

Preparation Time: 15 Minutes
Cooking Time: 3 hours
Servings: 4
Ingredients:

- 1 yellow bell pepper (Diced)
- Juice from 1 lime
- 1 red bell pepper (Diced)
- 1 medium onion (Diced)
- 1.5 teaspoon ground pepper
- 1 teaspoon cumin
- 2 garlic cloves (Diced)
- 1 cup salsa
- About 1.5 teaspoon sea salt
- 1 green pepper (Diced)
- 4 cups chicken broth
- 1/2 jalapeño pepper, diced
- 1 Tablespoon chili powder
- 1 teaspoon paprika
- 2 pounds chicken, boneless, skinless
- 1 teaspoon olive oil
- Garnish: sour cream, cilantro

Directions:

1. Rinse the chicken, pat dry. Dice into cubes. Place the ingredients in your pot starting with the salsa then vegetables, and jalapeno. Add the chicken. Add the seasoning.

2. Pour in the chicken broth. Cover and cook properly on low heat for about 3 hours. Test the chicken doneness. Cook longer if needed. Finally serve in bowls. Garnish with sour cream and cilantro.

65. Delightful Almond Butter Cups

Preparation Time: 10 Minutes
Cooking Time: 50 minutes
Servings: 1 dozen
Ingredients:
BASE:

- 2 tbsps. coconut butter
- Pinch of sea salt
- About 1.5 tsp pure maple syrup
- Pinch of cinnamon

- About 1/2 tsp pure vanilla extract
- 2 tbsps. coconut oil, melted
- 1/4 cup unsweetened cocoa powder

FOR THE FILLING:

- 1 tbsp coconut oil
- 1 pinch of sea salt
- About 1.5 tsp pure maple syrup
- 3 tbsps. almond butter

Directions:

1. First of all, whisk all the ingredients for the base in a mixing bowl. Put paper liners in a muffin baking tin, and spoon 1 teaspoon in each tin. Put in the fridge or freezer to set.
2. Mix all the ingredients for the filling and place in a pastry bag. Next, cut off a tiny corner of the bag with scissors. Take the cups from the fridge or freezer and add about 1/2 of the filling into the center of each cup, please cover with the base and then put back in the fringe or freezer.
3. Finally serve cold or at room temperature.

66. King sized Paleo Orange Chicken

Preparation Time: 15 minutes   **Cooking Time:** 15 minutes   **Servings:** 2
Ingredients:

- Salt and pepper

SAUCE:

- Orange juice – ½ cup
- Arrow root flour – 2 tbsps.
- Zest of large orange – 1
- Raw honey – 3 tbsps.

- Chicken thighs– 1 lb
- Dash of red pepper flakes
- Coconut aminos – 3.5 tbsps.
- Water – 1 cup
- Ground ginger – ½

- 4 tbsps. bacon fat

Directions:

1. First of all, season the chicken with pepper and sea salt, then set aside.
2. For the sauce, mix the ingredients in a saucepan and stir to combine.
3. Place the mixture over medium heat as you stir frequently. Allow the sauce to thicken and remove from heat. Heat bacon fat in a large skillet. Add the chicken, let it cook properly for about 5 to 10 minutes until browned. Drain excess fat from the pan and pour a portion of the sauce into the pan. Stir to coat the chicken. Remove from the heat and serve.

4. Finally pour the remaining portion of the sauce over some side steamed vegetables.

67. Pinnacle Thai Coconut Shrimp Curry

Preparation Time: 35 minutes
Cooking Time: 25 minutes
Servings: 3
Ingredients:
- Chopped scallions – 4
- Salt to taste
- Thai red curry paste – ½ tbsp.
- Fresh cilantro – 1/4 cup, chopped
- Garlic – 2 cloves, minced
- Fish sauce – 2 tsps.
- Shrimp – 1 lb. peeled and deveined
- Oil – about 1.5 tsp.
- Light coconut milk – 6 cups.

Directions:
1. First of all, heat oil over medium-high heat in a large skillet. Add scallion whites and curry paste and saute for about 2 minutes. Add garlic and shrimp. Season with salt and cook properly for about 2 to 5 minutes; then add fish sauce and coconut milk, mix well. Next, quickly simmer until shrimp is cooked through, about 3 to 5 minutes.
2. Remove from heat; mix in cilantro and scallion greens. Finally, serve over rice.

68. Tasty turkey Breasts Appetizer

Preparation Time: 15 minutes
Cooking Time: 2 hours
Servings: 6
Ingredients:
- 18 ounces Paleo apple jelly
- 2.5 pounds turkey breasts, sliced
- 9 ounces Dijon mustard

Directions:
1. First of all, place turkey breasts slices in your pot, add apple jelly and mustard and toss to coat really well. Cover and cook properly on low heat for about 2.5 hours stirring every 20 to 25 minutes. Finally arrange turkey breasts slices on a platter and serve.

69. Scrumptious Easy Chicken Casserole

Preparation Time: 30 Minutes
Cooking Time: 25 Minutes
Servings: 2
Ingredients:
- 1 Medium sweet potato (Diced)
- 1/2 tsp. Sea salt
- 4 eggs, whisked
- About 1 yellow onion (Diced)
- ½ tsp. garlic powder
- 1.5 tbsp. melted coconut oil
- 1 cup chopped spinach
- 250g Ground Chicken

Directions:
1. Preheat your oven to 400°F. Coat a 9x12 baking dish with Olive oil.
2. Toss the diced sweet potatoes and chopped spinach in coconut oil and sprinkle with salt; transfer to the baking sheet and then bake for about 25 to 30 minutes or until tender.
3. Meanwhile, set a sauté pan over medium heat; add yellow onion and sauté for about 2 to 5 minutes or until fragrant. Stir in chopped chicken and cook properly for about 5 to 7 minutes or until the chicken is no longer pink.
4. Next, quickly transfer the chicken to oven with the potatoes and spinach for about 30 minutes.
5. Finally, remove all from the oven. Top with garlic powder and salt. Serve.

70. Astonishing One Pot Super Spiced Meat

Preparation Time: minutes
Cooking Time: minutes
Servings: 2
Ingredients:

- Tomato paste – 3 tbsps.
- Crushed red pepper – 1/4 teaspoon
- Chili powder – about 1.5 tbsp.
- Paprika – 1/4 teaspoon
- Cumin – 1 tbsp.
- Black pepper – 1 tbsp.
- Onion powder – about 1 teaspoon
- Coriander – 1/2 tbsp.
- Dried oregano – 1/2 tbsp.
- Garlic powder – 1/2 teaspoon
- Grass fed ground beef – 2lbs

Directions:

1. First of all, combine the spices in a small bowl. Add beef, spices and tomato paste to the bowl and mix well the ingredients using a spoon as you also break up the meat.
2. Transfer all in a pot. Cook properly on low for about 1.5 hour as you break the meat further.
3. Remove the meat from the pot using a slotted spoon. Finally serve and enjoy.

71. Excellent Beef and Veggie Casserole

Preparation Time: 20 Minutes
Cooking Time: 30 Minutes
Servings: 2
Ingredients:

- 1 tbsp. extra virgin olive oil
- 3.5 tbsps. minced garlic
- Salt and pepper
- ½ cup diced onions
- ½ cup chopped fresh oregano
- 1 cup sliced purple cabbage
- 1.5 chopped red pepper
- 1 lb. ground beef

Directions:

1. Preheat your oven to 350°F. Brown beef in a saucepan; strain off fat and set aside.
2. Meanwhile, chop oregano, cabbage, garlic, onions, and pepper in a large bowl; set aside.
3. Grease a 9×13-inch baking dish with extra virgin olive oil and layer vegetables and hamburger until all ingredients are used. Next, quickly bake for about 20 to 25 minutes or until the vegetables are warmed but crunchy. Finally garnish with some dried Italian herbs, if you like.

72. Roasted Cabbage with Lime and Sriracha

Preparation Time: 25 minutes
Cooking Time: 45 minutes
Servings: 2
Ingredients:

- 2 tablespoons avocado oil
- 2 teaspoons sesame seeds
- 2 tablespoons lime juice
- 1/2 teaspoon sea salt
- 2.5 teaspoons Sriracha sauce
- 1 medium-sized head of firm cabbage

Directions:

1. Preheat the oven to 450°F and spray a baking sheet with non-stick spray or oil.

2. Remove outer leaves from the cabbage and cut it into quarters, same in size; then, cut each piece in half to get 8 wedges. Lay the cabbage wedges on the baking sheet, making sure they do not touch. Next, mix oil, Sriracha sauce, lime juice, and salt and brush the cabbage wedges with it on both sides leaving about 1/3 of the mixture. Place the baking sheet into the oven and then roast for 15 to 18 minutes, until the edges begin to brown; then carefully turn the wedges and brush with the remaining mixture. Roast for about 15 to 20 minutes more. Remove from the oven and trim of the core. Sprinkle with sesame seeds and serve hot.

73. Dashing Shrimp and Broccoli Feast

Preparation Time: 10 minutes
Cooking Time: 20 minutes
Servings: 4
Ingredients:

- 2 tablespoons ghee
- Pepper to taste
- 7 minced garlic cloves
- Juice of 1/2 lime
- 1 lb broccoli florets
- 1/4 cup chicken broth
- 1 bay leaf
- 1.5 teaspoon fish sauce
- 2/3 cup white wine
- 2 teaspoons toasted sesame oil
- 1.5 teaspoon red pepper flakes
- 1 lb peeled and deveined shrimp

Directions:

1. First of all, melt ghee in large pan over medium heat. Add garlic and sauté until softened.
2. Add the broccoli and other vegetables wanted, sautéing for about 2 minutes. Add shrimp and bay leaf. Increase heat to medium high and add red pepper flakes, sesame oil, and fish sauce.
3. Toss everything around in the pan to coat in the mixture. Cook properly for additional 2 to 5 minutes. Pour in broth and white wine, then reduce heat back to medium.
4. Let it cook properly for about 5 to 10 more minutes until the vegetables are soft and the shrimp is opaque. Finally squeeze lime juice over it and crack fresh pepper for taste, then serve!

74. Reliable Paleo One Pot Shredded Beef

Preparation Time: 10 minutes
Cooking Time: 4 to 5 hours
Servings: 6 to 8
Ingredients:

- 1/4 cup beef stock
- Salt and pepper
- About 1 Tablespoon oregano
- 2 Tablespoons tomato paste
- 1/4 teaspoon ancho Chile
- 1/2 teaspoon cumin
- About 1 teaspoon garlic
- 1/4 teaspoon cinnamon
- 1/4 teaspoon paprika
- 3.5 pounds chuck roast

Directions:

1. First of all, take a large pot and add meat, broth, and tomato paste. Stir the ingredients so the meat is coated. Sprinkle the seasoning over the meat.

2. Next, cover and cook on medium heat for about 4 to 5 hours. Stir frequently. Once the meat has finished cooking, use 2 forks to shred. Finally serve warm, on a bun or side with salad.

75. Yummy Shiitake Meat Loaf

Preparation Time: 30 minutes
Cooking Time: 1 hour 50 minutes
Servings: 5
Ingredients:

- 1/4 cup red wine
- 1/4 cup sliced shiitake mushrooms
- About 1 tsp garlic powder
- 2 plum tomatoes (Chopped)
- 1 omega 3 egg
- 1/2 tsp onion powder
- 1 tbsp extra virgin olive oil
- 1..5 tbsp freshly ground flaxseed
- 11/2 lbs ground grass-fed beef

Directions:

1. Preheat oven to 350°F.
2. Meanwhile, heat oil in a pan, add mushrooms and fry for about 5 to 10 minutes over medium heat. Add tomatoes and cook properly for about 5 to 10 minutes.
3. Remove all from the pan, let it rest for about 5 to 10 minutes; then put all in a blender.
4. Combine mixture with meat, spices, egg and flaxseed in a bowl, mix thoroughly and put in a loaf pan. Drizzle with red wine. Next, bake meatloaf for about 75 minutes.
5. Let it cool down for about 5 to 10 minutes before serving.

76. Spiced Flounder with Tomatoes

Preparation Time: 5 minutes
Cooking Time: 15 minutes

- Flounder fillets – 4 oozes pieces
- Cajun spice seasoning – about 1.5 tbsp.
- Onion – 3/4 cup, chopped
- Tomatoes – 2 and 1/2 cups (Chopped)

Servings: 2
Ingredients:

- Garlic – 2 cloves (Minced)
- Olive oil – about 1.5 tsp.
- Diced green bell pepper – 3/4 cup

Directions:

1. In a deep skillet, heat olive oil over medium heat. Cook properly onion and garlic until soft. Add spices, peppers, and tomatoes.
2. Cook on medium heat and stir for about 2 to 5 minutes, or until tomatoes are soft.
3. Place fillets in the sauce. Cover and cook properly on medium heat for about 10 to 15 minutes, or until fish flakes quickly. Place fish on plate and spoon sauce on top. Finally serve.

77. Cauliflower Rice with Lemon and Garlic

Preparation Time: 20 minutes
Cooking Time: 45 minutes
Servings: 2
Ingredients:

- 1 tablespoon olive oil
- 1.5 teaspoon fresh lemon juice
- 3 cloves garlic, hopped
- 2 teaspoons chopped parsley
- 1 teaspoon sea salt
- 16 oozes riced cauliflowers

Directions:

1. Make riced cauliflower by removing the core and cutting the cauliflower into florets; then add cauliflower in 3 or 4 batches to a food processor and pulse until the cauliflower resembles the

texture of rice or couscous, without over doing it.

2. Preheat the oven to about 410 to 420°F. Spray a large baking sheet with oil.

3. Chop garlic. Mix cauliflower with olive oil, garlic and salt. Spread the cauliflower on the prepared sheet in one layer and place into the oven. Bake for about 25 to 30 minutes. Stir after 10 to 15 minutes; then when golden, remove from the oven. While the cauliflower is roasting, squeeze lemon juice and chop fresh parsley.

4. Add lemon juice and parsley to the cauliflower rice. Enjoy!

78. Quick Cabbage Roll Ups

Preparation Time: 10 minutes
Cooking Time: 10 minutes
Servings: 2
Ingredients:

- 3.5 teaspoons pickling spice
- 2.5 teaspoons coconut oil
- Mustard (optional)
- ½ head of cabbage, leaves separated
- 1 lb grass-fed beef top sirloin
- Water

Directions:

1. First of all, heat a saucepan over medium high heat.

2. Next, place coconut oil, mustard, pickling spices, and any other wanted ingredients into the pan and combine. Add water as necessary to coat the bottom of the pan in the sauce.

3. Layer the cabbage leaves with cheese, meat, and any other vegetables you might enjoy, roll them, and secure it all together with a toothpick.

4. Set the cabbage rolls into the bubbling sauce and cook appropriately on both sides for about 5 to 10 minutes. Make sure the meat is cooked properly, then enjoy!

79. Wonderful Paleo Middle Eastern Beef

Preparation Time: 30 minutes
Cooking Time: 6 hours 5 minutes
Servings: 7
Ingredients:

- 1 teaspoon cloves
- Pinch of salt and pepper
- 1.5 teaspoon fennel seeds
- 1 teaspoon cumin powder
- ¼ cup coconut oil
- ½ teaspoon cloves
- ½ large sweet onion, diced
- 1 teaspoon cinnamon
- 1 teaspoon cardamom powder
- 3 cups bone broth
- 3 tablespoons tomato paste
- 3 pounds beef brisket, grass fed

Directions:

1. In a pot, season the meat with salt and pepper, then sprinkle mixture of cumin powder, fennel seeds, cloves. Add all the other ingredients. Cover and cook properly on medium for about 5 to 6 hours. Stir frequently. Shred with 2 forks once tender.

2. Put in a plate and side with rice. Serve warm.

80. Elegant Candied carrots

Preparation Time: 10 minutes
Cooking Time: 30 minutes
Servings: 4
Ingredients:

- Sea salt
- 4 pitted dates
- 8 large carrots
- 2.5 tbsps. melted butter

Directions:

1. First of all, peel and chop the carrots into 1/2-inch pieces, then chop the dates.
2. Put them in a baking dish, sprinkle with salt to taste and pour the melted butter on top.
3. Finally bake to 370°F for about 20 to 30 minutes.

81. Rich Zucchini pancakes

Preparation Time: 10 minutes
Cooking Time: 30 minutes
Servings: 3
Ingredients:

- 3 eggs
- Coconut oil
- 1.5 tbsp coconut flour
- Salt and pepper
- 1 big zucchini

Directions:

1. First of all, put zucchini in a blender. Whisk the eggs with the flour, salt and pepper. Add 2 cups of shredded zucchini and stir until well combined.
2. Heat coconut oil in a pan, then spoon the mixture to make medium pancakes. Cook properly over medium-low heat. Stir frequently. Finally, when slightly brown, flip on the other side.

82. Tasty Tomato Dill Frittata

Preparation Time: 10 to 15 Minutes
Cooking Time: 35 to 40 Minutes
Servings: 2 to 4
Ingredients:

- 2 tbsps. chopped dill
- Salt and pepper
- 2.5 tomatoes (Diced)
- 4 free-range eggs, whisked
- 1 tsp. red pepper flakes
- Coconut oil, for greasing the pan
- 2 garlic cloves (Minced)
- 2.5 tbsps. chopped fresh chives

Directions:

1. Preheat your oven to 320° F. Grease a cast iron skillet or saucepan and set aside.
2. In a medium or large bowl, please whisk together the eggs; beat in the remaining ingredients until well mixed; then quickly pour the egg mixture into the prepared pan and then bake for about 35 to 40 minutes or until cooked through.
3. Finally garnish the frittata with extra chives and dill to serve.

83. Yummy Chicken with Basil Avocado Cream Sauce

Preparation Time: 15 minutes
Cooking Time: 45 minutes
Servings: 2
Ingredients:
FOR THE CHICKEN:

- Italian seasoning, ½ teaspoon
- Salt and pepper to taste
- Onion powder, 1 teaspoon
- 4 chicken breasts

FOR THE AVOCADO SAUCE CREAM:

- Coconut milk – ½ cup
- Lemon Juice – 1 tablespoon

- Garlic cloves – 2
- Avocado – 1
- Fresh basil ½ cup

Directions:

1. Preheat the oven to 370°F. Place the chicken breasts in an 8x8 pan then top with olive oil.
2. Place the spices in a bowl then put 1/4 teaspoon of the herbs on each chicken breast. Bake the chicken for about 40 to 45 minutes or until well cooked. Set all the avocado cream sauce ingredients in a blender then mix until well blended. Add coconut milk for the desired consistency. Finally serve sauce with the chicken.

84. Unique Roasted Broccoli w/ Lemon

Preparation Time: 10 to 15 Minutes
Cooking Time: 20 to 30 Minutes
Servings: 3 to 4
Ingredients:

- 2 tsps. squeezed lemon juice
- A pinch of salt and pepper
- 2.5 tsps. grated lemon zest
- 4 minced cloves garlic
- 2 Heads of broccoli, chopped
- ½ cup extra virgin olive oil

Directions:

1. Preheat your oven to about 390 to 400°F. Place broccoli onto a rimmed baking sheet and drizzle with extra virgin olive oil; sprinkle with garlic, lemon zest, sea salt and pepper and toss to coat well.
2. Next bake for about 20 to 25 minutes, turning once, until broccoli florets are slightly browned.
3. Finally transfer the baked broccoli to a large bowl and toss with lemon juice. Serve warm.

85. Ultimate Beef, Cabbage, and Tomato Soup

Preparation Time: 20 minutes   **Cooking Time:** 50 minutes   **Servings:** 2
Ingredients:

- Salt and pepper
- Bay leaves – 2
- Diced onion – ½ cup
- Beef stock – 4 cups
- Diced celery – 1 cup
- Chopped green cabbage – 5 cups
- Diced carrot – ½ cup
- Diced tomatoes – 28 oozes can
- Lean ground beef – 1 lb. 90%
- 3 glass of water

Directions:

1. First of all, heat a large pot over medium-high heat. Spray with oil and add ground beef.
2. Season with salt and pepper and cook properly for about 2 to 5 minutes, or until browned.
3. Once browned, add celery, carrots, and onion and sauté for 5 minutes. Break the meat into smaller pieces. Add the bay leaves, cabbage, beef stock, and tomatoes. Stir and add water.
4. Finally cook properly on low heat for about 35 to 40 minutes, covered. Serve warm.

Fresh Paleo Meat Recipes

86. Lamb and Celery Casserole

Preparation Time: 10 minutes
Cooking Time: 45 minutes
Servings: 2
Ingredients:
- ¼ cup celery stalk, chopped
- 2 lamb chops, chopped
- ½ cup Mozzarella, shredded
- 1 teaspoon butter
- ¼ cup coconut cream
- 1 teaspoon taco seasonings

Directions:
1. Mix lamb chops with taco seasonings and put in the casserole mold.
2. Add celery stalk, coconut cream, and shredded mozzarella. Then add butter and cook the casserole in the preheated to 360°F oven for 45 minutes. Serve warm.

87. Lamb in Almond Sauce

Preparation Time: 10 minutes
Cooking Time: 30 minutes
Servings: 6
Ingredients:
- 14 oozes lamb fillet, cubed
- 1 cup organic almond milk
- 1 teaspoon almond flour
- 1 teaspoon ground nutmeg
- ½ teaspoon ground cardamom
- 1 tablespoon olive oil
- 1 tablespoon lemon juice
- 1 tablespoon butter
- ½ teaspoon minced garlic

Directions:
1. Take a pot and heat a bit of olive oil on low. Meanwhile, mix lamb, ground nutmeg, ground cardamom, and minced garlic. Put the lamb in the hot olive oil. Roast the meat for 2 minutes per side, and add butter, lemon juice, and almond milk. Carefully mix the mixture.
2. Cook the meal for 15 minutes on medium heat. Then add almond flour, stir well and simmer the meal for 10 minutes more. Serve immediately.

88. Sweet Leg of Lamb

Preparation Time: 10 minutes
Cooking Time: 45 minutes
Servings: 6
Ingredients:
- 2 pounds lamb leg
- 1 tablespoon Erythritol
- 3 tablespoons coconut milk
- 1 teaspoon chili flakes
- 1 teaspoon ground turmeric
- 1 teaspoon cayenne pepper
- 3 tablespoons coconut oil

Directions:
1. In the shallow bowl, mix cayenne pepper, ground turmeric, chili flakes, and Erythritol. Rub the lamb leg with spices. Melt the coconut oil in a pot. Add lamb leg and roast it for 10 minutes per side on low heat. After this, add coconut milk and cook the meal for 30 minutes on low heat. Stir frequently. Flip the meat on another side from time to time.

89. Coconut Lamb Shoulder

Preparation Time: 10 minutes   **Cooking Time:** 75 minutes

Servings: 5

Ingredients:
- 2-pound lamb shoulder
- 1 teaspoon ground cumin
- 2 tablespoons butter
- ¼ cup of coconut milk
- 1 teaspoon coconut shred
- ½ cup kale, chopped

Directions:
1. Put all ingredients in a pot (or saucepan) and mix well. Close the lid and cook the meal on low heat for 75 minutes. Stir frequently. Serve warm.

90. Lavender Lamb

Preparation Time: 10 minutes
Cooking Time: 35 minutes
Servings: 4
Ingredients:
- 4 lamb chops
- 1 teaspoon dried lavender
- 2 tablespoons butter
- 1 teaspoon cumin seeds
- 1 cup of water

Directions:
1. Toss the butter in the saucepan and melt it. Add lamb chops and roast them for 3 minutes. Then add dried lavender, cumin seeds, and water. Close the lid and cook the meat for 30 minutes on medium-low heat. Stir frequently. Serve warm.

91. Dill Lamb Shank

Preparation Time: 10 minutes
Cooking Time: 40 minutes
Servings: 3
Ingredients:
- 3 lamb shanks (4 oz each)
- 1 tablespoon dried dill
- 1 teaspoon peppercorns
- 3 cups of water
- 1 carrot, chopped
- 1 teaspoon salt

Directions:
1. Bring the water to boil. Add lamb shank, dried dill, peppercorns, carrot, and salt.
2. Close the lid and cook the meat in medium heat for 40 minutes. Stir properly. Serve warm.

92. Mexican Lamb Chops

Preparation Time: 10 minutes
Cooking Time: 15 minutes
Servings: 4
Ingredients:
- 4 lamb chops
- 1 tablespoon Mexican seasonings
- 2 tablespoons sesame oil
- 1 teaspoon butter

Directions:
1. Rub the lamb chops with Mexican seasonings. Then melt the butter in the skillet. Add sesame oil. Then add lamb chops and roast them for 7 minutes per side on medium heat. Serve.

93. Cilantro Garlic Pork Chops

Preparation Time: 10 Minutes
Cooking Time: 15 Minutes
Servings: 4
Ingredients:
- 2 pounds pork chopped
- Salt and pepper
- ¼ cup good-quality olive oil, divided
- ¼ cup finely chopped fresh cilantro
- 1 tablespoon minced garlic
- Juice of 1 lime

Directions:

1. Marinate the pork. Pat the pork chops dry and season them lightly with salt and pepper. Place them in a large bowl, add 2 tablespoons of the olive oil, and the cilantro, garlic, and lime juice.
2. Toss to coat the chops. Cover the bowl and marinate the chops at room temperature for 30 minutes. Cook the pork. In a large skillet over medium-high heat, warm the remaining 2 tablespoons of olive oil. Add the pork chops in a single layer and fry them, turning them once, until they're just cooked through and still juicy, 6 to 7 minutes per side.
3. Serve. Divide the chops between four plates and serve them immediately.

94. Spinach Feta Stuffed Pork

Preparation Time: 15 Minutes
Cooking Time: 30 Minutes
Servings: 4
Ingredients:

- 4 ounces crumbled feta cheese
- ¾ cup chopped frozen spinach
- 3 tablespoons chopped olives
- 4-ounce center pork chops, 2 inches thick
- Salt and pepper
- 3 tablespoons good-quality olive oil

Directions: Preheat the oven. Set the oven temperature to 400°F.

1. Make the filling. In a small bowl, mix together the feta, spinach, and olives until everything is well combined. Stuff the pork chops. Make a horizontal slit in the side of each chop to create a pocket, making sure you don't cut all the way through. Stuff the filling equally between the chops and secure the slits with toothpicks. Lightly season the stuffed chops with salt and pepper. Brown the chops. In a large oven-safe skillet over medium-high heat, warm the olive oil. Add the chops and sear them until they're browned all over, about 10 minutes in total.
2. Roast the chops. Place the skillet in the oven and roast the chops for 20 minutes or until they're cooked through. Serve. Let the meat rest for 10 minutes and then remove the toothpicks. Divide the pork chops between four plates and serve them immediately.

95. Coconut Milk Ginger Marinated Pork Tenderloin

Preparation Time: 5 Minutes   **Cooking Time:** 25 Minutes   **Servings:** 4
Ingredients:

- ¼ cup coconut oil, divided
- 1½ pounds boneless pork chopped
- 1 tablespoon grated fresh ginger
- 2 teaspoons minced garlic
- 1 cup coconut milk
- 1 teaspoon chopped basil
- Juice of 1 lime
- ½ cup shredded coconut

Directions:

1. Brown the pork. In a large skillet over medium heat, warm 2 tablespoons of the coconut oil. Add the pork chops to the skillet and brown them all over, turning them several times, about 10 minutes in total.
2. Braise the pork. Move the pork to the side of the skillet and add the remaining 2 tablespoons of coconut oil. Add the ginger and garlic and sauté until they've softened, about 2 minutes. Stir in the coconut milk, basil, and lime juice and move the pork back to the center of the skillet. Cover the skillet and simmer until the pork is just cooked through and very tender, 12 to 15 minutes. Serve the pork chops between four plates and top them with the shredded coconut.

96. Grilled Pork Chops with Greek Salsa

Preparation Time: 15 Minutes
Cooking Time: 15 Minutes
Servings: 4
Ingredients:

- ¼ cup olive oil, divided
- 1 tablespoon red wine
- 3 teaspoons chopped oregano, divided
- 1 teaspoon minced garlic
- 4-ounce boneless pork chopped
- ½ cup halved cherry tomatoes
- ½ yellow bell pepper, diced
- ½ English cucumber, chopped
- ¼ red onion, chopped
- 1 tablespoon balsamic vinegar
- Salt and pepper for seasoning

Directions:

1. Marinate the pork. In a medium bowl, stir together 3 tablespoons of the olive oil, the wine, 2 teaspoons of the oregano, and the garlic. Add the pork chops to the bowl, turning them to get them coated with the marinade. Cover the bowl and place it in the refrigerator for 30 minutes.
2. Make the salsa. While the pork is marinating, in a medium bowl, stir together the remaining 1 tablespoon of olive oil, the tomatoes, yellow bell pepper, cucumber, red onion, vinegar, and the remaining 1 teaspoon of oregano. Season the salsa with salt and pepper. Set the bowl aside.
3. Grill the pork chops. Heat a grill to medium-high heat. Remove the pork chops from the marinade and grill them until just cooked through, 6 to 8 minutes per side.
4. Serve. Rest the pork for 5 minutes. Divide the pork between four plates and serve them with a generous scoop of the salsa.

97. Grilled Herbed Pork Kebabs

Preparation Time: 10 Minutes
Cooking Time: 15 Minutes
Servings: 4
Ingredients:

- ¼ cup good-quality olive oil
- 1 tablespoon minced garlic
- 2 teaspoons dried oregano
- 1 teaspoon dried basil
- 1 teaspoon dried parsley
- Salt and pepper to taste
- 1-pound pork tenderloin, chopped

Directions:

1. Marinate the pork. In a medium bowl, stir together the olive oil, garlic, oregano, basil, parsley, salt, and pepper. Add the pork pieces and toss to coat them in the marinade. Cover the bowl and place it in the refrigerator for 2 to 4 hours.
2. Make the kebabs. Divide the pork pieces between four skewers, making sure not to crowd the meat. Grill the kebabs. Preheat your grill to medium-high heat. Grill the skewers for about 12 minutes, turning to cook all pork sides until the pork is cooked through.
3. Serve. Rest the skewers for 5 minutes. Divide the skewers between four plates and serve them immediately.

98. Pork Meat and Broccoli Sauté

Preparation Time: 10 Minutes
Cooking Time: 20 Minutes
Servings: 4
Ingredients:

- 2 tablespoons olive oil
- 2 pounds pork meat
- 4 cups small broccoli florets
- 1 tablespoon minced garlic
- Black pepper to taste

Directions:

1. Cook the sausage. In a large skillet over medium heat, warm the olive oil. Add the chop pork meat sauté it until it's cooked through, 8 to 10 minutes. Transfer the meat to a plate with a slotted spoon and set the plate aside. Sauté the vegetables. Add the broccoli to the skillet and sauté it until it's tender, about 6 minutes. Stir in the garlic and sauté for another 3 minutes.
2. Finish the dish. Return the meat to the skillet and toss to combine it with the other ingredients. Season the mixture with pepper.
3. Serve. Divide the mixture between four plates and serve it immediately.

99. Lemon-Infused Pork Rib Roast

Preparation Time: 10 Minutes
Cooking Time: 1 Hour
Servings: 6
Ingredients:
- ¼ cup good-quality olive oil
- Zest and juice of 1 lemon
- Zest and juice of 1 orange
- 4 rosemary sprigs, lightly crushed
- 4 thyme sprigs, lightly crushed
- 4-bone pork rib roast
- 6 garlic cloves, peeled
- Salt and pepper for seasoning

Directions:
1. Make the marinade. In a large bowl, combine the olive oil, lemon zest, lemon juice, orange zest, orange juice, rosemary sprigs, and thyme sprigs.
2. Marinate the roast. Use a small knife to make six 1-inch-deep slits in the fatty side of the roast. Stuff the garlic cloves in the slits. Put the roast in the bowl with the marinade and turn it to coat it well with the marinade. Cover the bowl and refrigerate it overnight, turning the roast in the marinade several times.
3. Preheat the oven. Set the oven temperature to 350°F.
4. Roast the pork. Remove the pork from the marinade and season it with salt and pepper, then put it in a baking dish and let it come to room temperature. Roast the pork until it's cooked through (145°F to 160°F internal temperature), about 1 hour. Throw out any leftover marinade.
5. Serve. Let the pork rest for 10 minutes, then cut it into slices and arrange the slices on a platter. Serve it warm.

100. Greek Beef Stew

Servings: 8
Cooking Time: 8 hours
Ingredients
- 4 pounds meat beef
- 20 whole shallots, peeled
- 3 bay leaves
- 8 garlic cloves
- 3 sprigs rosemary
- 6 whole pimento
- 5 whole cloves
- 1/2 teaspoon ground nutmeg
- 1/2 cup avocado oil
- 1/3 cup apple cider vinegar
- Salt and pepper
- 2 cups tomato paste

Instructions
Put all ingredients in the slow cooker and cook on low for 8 hours.

101. Chipotle Lamb Ribs

Preparation Time: 15 minutes
Cooking Time: 20 minutes
Servings: 6
Ingredients:

- 2-pound lamb ribs
- 1 tablespoon chipotle pepper, minced
- 2 tablespoons sesame oil
- 1 teaspoon apple cider vinegar

Directions:
1. Mix lamb ribs with all ingredients and leave to marinate for 10 minutes.
2. Then transfer the lamb ribs and all marinade in the baking tray and cook the meat in the oven at 360°F for 40 minutes. Flip the ribs on another side after 20 minutes of cooking.

102. Lamb and Pecan Salad

Preparation Time: 10 minutes
Cooking Time: 10 minutes
Servings: 4
Ingredients:
- 2 lamb chops
- 1 tablespoon sesame oil
- 2 pecans, chopped
- 2 cups lettuce, chopped
- 1 teaspoon cayenne pepper
- 1 tablespoon avocado oil

Directions:
1. Sprinkle the lamb chops with cayenne pepper and put in the hot skillet.
2. Add sesame oil and roast the meat for 4 minutes per side. Then chops the lamb chops and put them in the salad bowl. Add all remaining ingredients and carefully mix the salad.

103. Hot Sauce Lamb

Preparation Time: 10 minutes
Cooking Time: 35 minutes
Servings: 4
Ingredients:
- 2 teaspoons paprika
- pound lamb fillet, chopped
- 1 tablespoon coconut oil
- 4 tablespoons keto hot sauce
- ½ cup of water

Directions:
1. Pour water in the saucepan and bring it to boil. Add lamb and boil it for 20 minutes.
2. After this, preheat the skillet well. Add boiled lamb fillet, coconut oil, and paprika.
3. Roast the ingredients for 6 minutes per side or until the meat is light brown. Then add hot sauce and carefully mix the meal. Serve.

104. Mustard Lamb Chops

Prep. Time: 10 minutes
Cooking Time: 40 minutes
Servings: 4
  Ingredients:
- 1 cup spinach
- 3 tablespoons mustard
- 2 tablespoons sesame oil
- ½ teaspoon turmeric
- 4 lamb chops

Directions:
1. Blend the spinach and mix it with mustard, sesame oil, and ground turmeric.
2. Rub the lamb chops with the mustard mixture and put in the baking pan.
3. Bake the meat at 355F for 40 minutes. Flip the meat after 20 minutes of cooking. Serve.

105. Ginger Lamb Chops

Preparation Time: 15 minutes
Cooking Time: 30 minutes
Servings: 6
Ingredients:
- 6 lamb chops
- 1 tablespoon keto tomato paste
- 1 teaspoon minced ginger

- 2 tablespoons avocado oil
- 1 teaspoon plain yogurt

Directions:

1. Mix plain yogurt with keto tomato paste and minced ginger.
2. Then put the lamb chops in the yogurt mixture and marinate for 10-15 minutes.
3. After this, transfer the mixture in the tray, add avocado oil, and cook the meat at 360°F in the oven for 30 minutes. Serve warm.

106. Parmesan Lamb

Preparation Time: 10 minutes
Cooking Time: 20 minutes
Servings: 4
Ingredients:

- 4 lamb chops
- 2 cups Parmesan, grated
- ½ cup plain yogurt
- 3 scallions, sliced
- 1 tablespoon butter, softened

Directions:

1. Melt the butter in the saucepan. Add scallions and roast it for 3-4 minutes. Then stir the scallions and add lamb chops. Roast them for 2 minutes per side. Add yogurt and close the lid. Cook the meat for 10 minutes.
2. After this, top the meat with Parmesan and cook it for 2 minutes more. Serve warm.

107. Clove Lamb

Preparation Time: 10 minutes
Cooking Time: 25 minutes
Servings: 4
Ingredients:

- 1 teaspoon ground clove
- 2 tablespoons butter
- 1 teaspoon ground paprika
- 1 teaspoon dried rosemary
- ¼ cup of water
- 12 oozes lamb fillet

Directions:

1. In the shallow bowl, mix ground clove with ground paprika, and dried rosemary.
2. Rub the lamb fillet with spices and grease with butter. Then put the meat in the hot skillet and roast it for 5 minutes per side on the low heat. Add water. Close the lid and cook the lamb on medium heat for 15 minutes. Serve warm.

108. Carrot Lamb Roast

Preparation Time: 10 minutes
Cooking Time: 40 minutes

- 1-pound lamb loin
- 1 carrot, chopped
- 1 teaspoon dried thyme
- 2 tablespoons coconut oil
- 1 teaspoon salt

Servings:4
Ingredients:

Directions:

1. Put all ingredients in the baking tray and mix well. Bake the mixture in the preheated to 360°F oven for 40 minutes. Serve warm.

109. Beef, Parsnip, Celery Stew

Servings: 8

Cooking Time: 8 hours

Ingredients

- 3 pounds beef meat
- 2 chopped onions
- 6 chopped carrots
- 2 tablespoons olive oil
- 1 sprig dried thyme
- 2 chopped parsnips
- 1/2 cup brown rice
- 4 cups beef stock
- Salt and black pepper
- 1 bunch chopped parsley
- 1 bunch chives

Instructions

Put all ingredients in the slow cooker and cook on low for 8 hours.

110. Beef meat with Red Beans

Servings: 6
Cooking Time: 4 hours

Ingredients

- 3 tablespoons olive oil
- 1 chopped onion
- 1 lb cubed beef meet
- 2 teaspoons ground cumin
- 2 teaspoon turmeric
- 1 teaspoon cinnamon
- 3 cups water
- 4 tablespoons chopped fresh parsley
- 3 tablespoons snipped chives
- 2 cups cooked kidney beans
- 3 tablespoons lemon juice
- Salt and pepper to taste

Instructions

Put all ingredients in the pot and cook on low for 4 hours.

Paleo Desserts and Snacks

111. Unique Banana Pancakes

Preparation Time: 5 to 10 Minutes

Cooking Time: 15 minutes

Servings: 2 to 4

Ingredients:

- Vanilla Extract, dash (Optional)
- 1 free-range egg
- About 1.5 tsp cinnamon
- 1 tsp of coconut (Shredded)
- 1 banana (Mashed)
- Seeds for garnish (Optional)

Directions:

1. Mash one whole banana and lightly beat with an egg.
2. For extra flavor, add coconut chips, vanilla extract (just a dash) and cinnamon. Put this in a pan with a bit of oil on the bottom (or pour this mixture into a frying pan, if you have) and cook properly as you would a regular pancake.
3. Serve with garnish. Enjoy!

112. Awesome Safe Blueberry Muffin

Preparation Time: 15 Minutes

Cooking Time: 25 minutes

Servings: 2 to 4

Ingredients:

- 1 teaspoon coconut flour
- 3 tablespoons cinnamon
- ½ teaspoon baking soda
- 3/4 cup fresh blueberries
- 1/4 teaspoon salt
- 1/2 tablespoon vanilla
- 2 eggs
- 1/4 cup coconut oil
- 1/2 cup maple syrup
- 2 cups almond flour
- 1/3 cup coconut milk

Directions:

1. Preheat the oven to 350° F. Line a muffin tin and oil it up with coconut oil.
2. Combine flours, salt, and baking soda in a mixing bowl. Pour in eggs, maple syrup, coconut oil, coconut milk, and vanilla; then mix well. Gently fold in the blueberries and cinnamon, careful not to fold the mixture more than 10 times. Pour into muffin tin and sprinkle with extra cinnamon. Finally bake for about 20 to 25 minutes before allowing to cool. Then, enjoy!

113. Crazy Almond Joy Ice Cream

Preparation Time: 35 minutes

Cooking Time: 15 minutes

Servings: 3

Ingredients:

- ½ cup honey
- ½ cup unsweetened coconut flakes
- ½ tablespoon vanilla extract
- ¼ cup sliced almonds
- 1 dark baking chocolate bar
- 2 ½ cans full fat coconut milk

Directions:

1. In a blender, mix together the honey, coconut milk, and vanilla extract.
2. Now line a plastic container with plastic wrap. Pour the mixture into it and freeze it overnight.
3. The next day, take half of the frozen mixture and please add it to a food processor; quickly mix it on high until it resembles frozen yogurt and then put it back into a storage container.
4. Repeat this process with the other half of the mixture.
5. Return the blended ice cream to the freeze for about 30 to 35 minutes before serving.
6. To assemble, quickly melt the chocolate chips in a saucepan over low heat, to safely prevent burning the chocolate.
7. Serve each Almond Joy Sunday with a scoop of the ice cream. Finally drizzle the melted chocolate on top, then sprinkle with coconut flakes and sliced almonds. Serve immediately.

114. Charming Blueberry lemon muffins

Preparation Time: 20 minutes

Cooking Time: 40 minutes

Servings: 12

Ingredients:

- ½ cup coconut oil
- 1 cup fresh blueberries
- ½ tsp pure vanilla extract
- ¼ tsp baking soda
- ¼ cup grade B maple syrup
- About 1 tsp salt
- 1 lemon, juice and zest
- ½ cup flour

- 6 eggs

Directions:

1. First of all, melt coconut oil. Next, mix the eggs, maple syrup, pure vanilla extract, lemon juice, and lemon zest and melted coconut oil. Sift in the salt, flour, and baking soda, and blend until smooth. Add the blueberries. Stir properly. Fill 3/4 of the batter into the baking silicon cups.
2. Finally bake for about 35 to 40 minutes to 350°F. Serve.

115. Sweet potato pancakes

Preparation Time: 20 minutes

Cooking Time: 20 minutes

Servings: 4

Ingredients:

- 3 eggs
- Pinch salt
- 15ml coconut oil
- 1/2 teaspoon rosemary
- 2 teaspoons coconut flour
- 5 sweet potatoes

Directions:

1. First of all, wash sweet potatoes, dry them with paper towels. Chop finely.
2. Pre-heat the skillet over medium-low heat, pout coconut oil.
3. Beat eggs in a mixing bowl with coconut flour, rosemary and salt. Add chopped sweet potatoes and mix thoroughly. Next, put the spoonful of the mixture on the skillet, cook properly for about 2 to 5 minutes on one side, toss and cook properly 2 more minutes.
4. Do it until there is no mixture left. Finally put the pancakes on the plate. Serve with garnish.

116. Elegant Shrimp Avocado Salad

Preparation Time: 5 minutes

Cooking Time: 5 minutes

Servings: 6

Ingredients:

- Pinch salt and pepper
- 100g cherry tomatoes
- 1/2 onion
- Pinch oregano
- 60ml olive oil
- 4 tbsps. chopped cilantro
- 2.5 teaspoons hot sauce
- 2 avocados
- 2 oranges
- 4 tablespoons lime juice
- 2.5 tablespoons chopped mint
- 2 tablespoons cooking fat
- 24 colossal shrimps

Directions:

1. Pre-heat a grill pan over high heat, add cooking fat.
2. Wash shrimps, then peel them off and devein. Mix olive oil, lime juice, hot sauce and mint in the bowl. Plunge shrimps in the mixture and place them on the grill pan. Fry for about 2 to 5 minutes on each side. Meanwhile wash avocados, oranges and tomatoes, dry them with paper towels. Cut tomatoes into halves, avocados into wedges and oranges into segments. Slice the onion and put it in the bowl with mixture together with oranges, tomatoes, avocados, cilantro and oregano. Mix well and put in the plates. Finally add grilled shrimps to the plates.

117. Quick Strawberries with Crème

Preparation Time: 20 minutes
Cooking Time: 40 minutes
Servings: 5
Ingredients:

- 1 tsp vanilla extract
- 2 cups sliced fresh strawberries
- ½ cup fresh coconut milk

Directions:

1. First of all, put a whisk and a copper bowl in the freezer for about 30 to 35 minutes before cooking. Put strawberries and vanilla in a bowl and stir gently. Cover and put in the fridge for 35 minutes. Next, pour coconut milk into the copper bowl and whisk until thickens slightly.
2. Finally place strawberries in individual dishes and cover with the crème. Enjoy!

118. Delightful Banana Dessert

Preparation Time: 15 minutes
Cooking Time: 40 minutes
Servings: 2
Ingredients:

- 4 tbsps. pecans
- Freshly ground nutmeg
- 1.5 tsp pure vanilla extract
- ¼ tsp ground allspice
- ½ tsp ground ginger
- 2 large ripe bananas

Directions:

1. Cut bananas in half lengthwise. Meanwhile, mix vanilla, ginger, and allspice in a small jar and shake well. Brush the mixture over bananas and put them cut side down on wax paper. Leave in freezer for 35 minutes. Toast pecans and chop finely. Finally garnish bananas with the pecans and sprinkle with nutmeg.

119. Awesome Spiced Orange Glazed Ham

Preparation Time: 40 minutes
Cooking Time: 2 hours 10 minutes
Servings: 1 to 2
Ingredients:

- 10 pounds cooked raw ham
- 3 tablespoons maple syrup

FOR THE RUB:

- 2 teaspoons onion powder
- ½ teaspoon cayenne
- ½ teaspoon smoked paprika
- ½ teaspoon cinnamon
- ½ teaspoon ground cloves
- ½ teaspoon garlic powder

FOR THE GLAZE:

- ½ cup coconut aminos
- 1 teaspoon chili powder
- 2 ½ tablespoons maple syrup
- ½ teaspoon smoked paprika
- ½ teaspoon fish sauce
- 2 cups orange juice
- Zest of about ½ orange
- FOR GARNISH:
- 4 navel oranges, cut in half

Directions: Preheat oven to 320 °F.

1. Combine onion powder, garlic powder, smoked paprika, ground clove, cinnamon, and cayenne. Put the raw ham into a pan and cover with the maple syrup. Rub the spice mixture onto the ham, completely covering it and letting it get between the slices.
2. Cover the ham with foil, put into the oven and bake for about 1.5 hours. Then half an hour before the ham is done, add orange juice, coconut aminos, orange zest, maple syrup, fish sauce, smoked paprika and chili powder into a large pan and mix well. Cook over medium heat for about 25

minutes, stirring frequently. When it is reduced by 1/3 and begins to boil, remove from heat. Remove foil from the ham, when done, and glaze the entire ham with half of the prepare orange glaze. Stick a few toothpicks through the ham to prevent unfolding and put orange halve around. Next, put the ham back into the oven and cook properly for about 30 to 35 more minutes at 400°F. Remove and glaze with the rest of the orange glaze. Finally serve.

120. Elegant Chocolate Orange and Mint Chip Truffles

Preparation Time: 10 minutes
Cooking Time: 25 to 30 minutes
Servings: 1 dozen truffles
Ingredients:
BASE:

- 6.5 tbsps. coconut butter
- ½ tsp pure vanilla extract
- 4 tbsps. coconut oil
- 4 tbsps. almond butter

MINT CHIP FLAVOR:

- 1 tsp pure maple syrup

- 2.5 tsps. mint extract
- 1 tbsp cacao nibs

FOR THE COATING:

- 2 tbsps. cacao powder
- Chocolate orange flavor:
- 2 tsps. pure maple syrup
- 2.5 tbsps. cocoa powder
- Zest of one orange
- 2 tbsps. shredded coconut
- About 1.5 tsp orange zest

Directions:

1. First of all, put the coconut oil, pure vanilla extract, coconut and almond butter into a bowl, and stir until well combined. Split the base in half add ingredients for mint chip flavor to one half, and ingredients for chocolate orange flavor to another half. Stir both mixtures thoroughly.
2. Next, put both mixtures in the freezer for about 10 to 15 minutes.
3. Form 1-inch balls with your hands and roll each one in the coating for its flavor. Finally place the balls on a plate and put in the fridge until solid.

121. Rich Omelet Under Applesauce

Preparation Time: 15 minutes
Cooking Time: 30 minutes
Servings: 1 dozen truffles
Ingredients:

- ½ teaspoon dash vanilla
- 2-3 strawberries
- ½ teaspoon cinnamon
- 2 tablespoons applesauce
- 3-4 eggs

Directions:

1. First of all, if you don't have applesauce, take 1/2 apple, remove the core and the skin, fine grate the rest to get the applesauce. Slice the strawberries.
2. Pre-heat the skillet over medium heat.

3. Break the eggs into the bowl, add cinnamon and vanilla, stir thoroughly. Then pour the mixture on the skillet, cook it properly for about 2 to 5 minutes till it mostly ready, toss it.

4. Cook it properly for about 2 minutes, transfer it on the plate. Finally distribute the applesauce over the half of the omelet, add strawberry, fold it with another half and cut into 2 portions.

122. Titanic Apple Butter

Preparation Time: 15 minutes
Cooking Time: 8 hours
Servings: 10
Ingredients:

- 1 teaspoon allspice
- 1 cup maple syrup
- 1.5 teaspoon clove
- 1/4 teaspoon nutmeg
- 1 teaspoon ginger powder
- 1 and 1/2 cups water
- 3 pounds apples, peeled
- 1.5 tablespoon cinnamon
- Juice of 1 lemon

Directions:

1. In your pot, mix apples with water, lemon juice, allspice, cinnamon, clove, ginger powder, maple syrup and nutmeg. Cover and cook properly on low heat for about 7 to 8 hours. Stir frequently. Then leave your mix to cool down for about 10 to 15 minutes, blend using an immersion blender and pour into small jars. Serve (also for garnish).

123. Rich Simple Breakfast Meatloaf

Preparation Time: 15 minutes
Cooking Time: 3 hours 20 minutes
Servings: 4 to 6
Ingredients:

- 2 pounds pork, minced
- 2 eggs
- 1.5 teaspoon red pepper flakes
- 1 teaspoon marjoram, dried
- 1 teaspoon coconut oil
- 1 tablespoon paprika
- 3 garlic cloves (Minced)
- 1/4 cup almond flour
- A pinch of sea salt
- 1.5 teaspoon oregano, minced
- 1 tablespoon sage, minced
- 1 onion, chopped

Directions:

1. First of all, heat up a pan with the oil over medium high heat, add onion, stir and cook properly for about 2 to 5 minutes. Add garlic, stir, cook properly for about 2 to 5 minutes more, take off heat and leave aside to cool down.

2. In a bowl, mix pork with a pinch of salt, pepper flakes, flour, paprika, oregano, sage, marjoram and eggs and whisk everything. Next, add garlic and onion and stir again. Shape your meatloaf, transfer to your pot, cover and cook properly on low for about 3.5 hours. Stir frequently.

3. Finally leave aside to cool down, slice and serve.

124. Titanic Paleo Strawberry Clementine Smoothie

Preparation Time: 10 minutes

Cooking Time: 0 minutes

Servings: 2

Ingredients:

- 1.5 banana, frozen, chopped into chunks
- 8 oozes strawberries – frozen or fresh
- 2 Clementines or Mandarins

Directions:

1. First of all, thaw the frozen banana chunks for at least 5 to 10 minutes.
2. Slightly defrost the frozen strawberries; then in the meantime, peel clementines and remove seeds. Finally combine all the ingredients in a blender and pulse until very smooth.
3. Put the mix in a cup and serve with garnish if you want.

125. Tasty Paleo Breakfast Burrito

Preparation Time: 5 to 10 minutes

Cooking Time: 5 to 10 minutes

Servings: 1 to 3

Ingredients:

- Eggs – 2
- Salsa guacamole (optional)
- Chopped vegetables
- 1 cup spinach,
- 4 black olives,
- 1 bell pepper, chopped
- 1 tomato, chopped
- Sliced meat fat - 2

Directions:

1. Over medium heat, sauté the veggies in a bit of oil for about 2 to 5 minutes.
2. Meanwhile, in a bowl whisk the eggs then pour the mixed vegetables. Use a spatula to scramble the mixture until cooked through. Remove the eggs from the pan then have them rolled around the fat slices; then return them back to the skillet. Grill for about 30 to 40 seconds or until the fat slices turns slightly brown. Finally, you can serve it with guacamole, salsa or fresh cilantro topping.

126. Yummy Cucumber and Tomato Salad

Preparation Time: 20 minutes

Cooking Time: 0 minutes

Servings: 5

Ingredients:

- 1 tsp black pepper
- 1 cup olives
- 1.5 tbsp. fresh Basil, sliced
- 2 tbsps. Olive Oil
- 1 tbsp. oregano, minced
- 2.5 tbsps. Balsamic Vinegar
- 2 cups Cucumber, chopped
- 2 cups Grape Tomatoes
- 1 clove Garlic, minced

Directions:

1. First of all, rinse and peel cucumber. Use julienne peeler to make noodles from the flesh of the cucumber. Stop when you get down to the seeds; then rinse grape tomatoes, slice in half. Thinly slice basil, chop oregano, and mince garlic. Finally toss all ingredients with the Kalamata olives in a medium mixing bowl, drizzle with olive oil and balsamic vinegar, and sprinkle with pepper.

127. Unique Turkey Taco Lettuce Wraps

Preparation Time: 10 minutes

Cooking Time: 25 minutes

Servings: 5

Ingredients:

- Garlic powder – 1 tsp.
- Reduced fat cheddar ½ cup
- Cumin – about 1.5 tsp.
- Iceberg lettuce leaves – 8
- Salt – 1 tsp.
- Chili powder – 1 tsp.
- Tomato sauce – 4 oozes
- Paprika – 1 tsp.
- Oregano –1 tsp.
- Water – 3/4 cup
- Small onion – ½, minced
- Bell pepper – ¼ minced
- Lean ground turkey – 1.3 lbs.

Directions:

1. In a large skillet, brown turkey on low heat and break it into smaller pieces. Once it browned, add dry seasoning and mix well. Add tomato sauce, pepper, water, onion, and cover. Simmer for about 25 minutes, on low. Finally divide the meat among 8 leaves and top with cheese.

128. Ultimate Pan-Fried Lemon Chicken

Preparation Time: 15 minutes
Cooking Time: 15 minutes
Servings: 5
Ingredients:

- Zest and juice of 1 lemon
- Fat of choice
- 1.5 teaspoons olive oil
- Salt and pepper
- 1 chicken breast

Directions:

1. Zest the lemon and squeeze the juice. Add chicken breast, olive oil, lemon zest and juice, salt and pepper to a cooking-zip lock bag. Seal the bag, squeezing out the air.
2. Then, flatten the chicken with a meat pounder or maybe rolling pin, so it is even in thickness.
3. Set it aside for about 30 to 35 minutes or cook immediately; then add oil or other fat of choice to a skillet and heat over medium-high heat. Remove the chicken from the bag and add to the skillet. Fry the chicken on both sides for about 2 to 5 minutes on each or until cooked.
4. Wait about 5 to 10 minutes before slicing. Serve!

129. Iconic Chocolate Granola

Preparation Time: 15 minutes
Cooking Time: 30 minutes
Servings: 4
Ingredients:

- 2.5 tablespoons rice malt syrup
- 2/3 cup raisins
- 1/2 cup cocoa powder
- 2/3 cup pumpkin seeds
- 1/2 cup coconut flakes
- 2/3 cup chopped nuts
- 2.5 ounces coconut oil

Directions:

1. Preheat oven to 150°F.
2. Melt coconut oil (or butter) in a saucepan, then add rice malt syrup and cocoa powder. Stir until well blended. Combine coconut flakes and nuts in a bowl; then, pour cocoa syrup mixture on top

and toss until lightly coated. Next, spread mixture on a baking sheet covered in tin foil. Place into the oven for about 25 to 30 minutes, stirring every 10 to 15 minutes. Stop when the coconut is well-browned.

3. Remove from the oven and allow to cool. Finally, if desired, pour some coconut milk over top and eat it like cereal!

130. Awesome Paleo Slow Cooker Sweet Potato Chipotle Chili

Preparation Time: 40 minutes
Cooking Time: 5 hour 5 minutes
Servings: 6
Ingredients:

- 2 cups chicken or beef broth
- 1 teaspoon paprika
- 3 sweet potatoes, chopped
- 3 cups cauliflower, chopped
- Salt and pepper
- 1 white onion, chopped
- ½ red onion, chopped
- ½ teaspoon cumin
- 2 chipotle peppers, minced
- 2 garlic cloves, minced
- 14-ounce can dice tomatoes
- pound ground beef, or chicken
- Shallots or parsley for garnish

Directions:

1. First of all, place the meat of choice, peppers, cauliflower, potatoes, white onions only, garlic, and diced tomatoes in your pot. Pour in the broth and heat on low for 10 minutes. Stir well.
2. Cover and cook properly on high for about 3 to 4 hours, stirring occasionally. Add red onions last hour of cooking. Serve in bowls. Garnish with shallots or parsley.

131. Mighty Paleo Crock Pot Beef Stew

Preparation Time: 30 minutes
Cooking Time: 6 hours 10 minutes
Servings: 6
Ingredients:

- 3 carrots, chopped
- Salt and pepper, each
- 1 cup peas, frozen
- 1 bay leaf
- 2 celery stalks, chopped
- 1.5 tablespoon tapioca flour
- 1 teaspoon thyme
- 1 large onion, chopped
- 2 garlic cloves, minced
- 3 cups beef broth
- 1.5 teaspoon parsley
- 1 cup chopped mushrooms
- 2 tablespoons tomato paste
- 1 tablespoon paprika
- 2 pounds ground chuck, boneless
- 1 Tablespoon garlic powder

Directions:

1. Add the meat, vegetables and flour to the pot. Stir together to coat ingredients. Stir in the onion, celery, garlic cloves, peas and seasoning. Add the broth, tomato paste. Stir well. Cover and cook properly on low for approximately 7 to 8 hours. Stir occasionally. If the mixture seems dry, quickly add more broth. Take out the bay leaf. Finally serve in bowls.

132. King sized Cherry-Berry Medley

Preparation Time: 20 minutes
Cooking Time: 40 minutes
Servings: 4
Ingredients:

- 1/2 cup blueberries
- 4 chopped mint leaves
- ½ cup golden raspberries
- ½ tsp ground cinnamon
- ½ cup blackberries
- 1 tsp clove powder
- 1 tsp vanilla extract
- 1/2 cup bing/rainier cherries

Directions:

1. Pit and chop the cherries. Combine all the berries in a bowl, add spices and chopped mint and toss gently; then chill for about 30 to 35 minutes. Garnish with mint leaves and serve

133. Crazy Bacon wrapped sausages

Preparation Time: 25 minutes
Cooking Time: 45 minutes
Servings: 6
Ingredients:

- 12 rashers bacon
- Salt and pepper
- 2 eggs
- 130 ml olive oil
- 3 tablespoons mustard
- 120 ml coconut oil
- 12 pork sausages
- 3.5 teaspoons lemon juice

Directions:

1. Pre-heat an oven over medium heat, cover the baking dish with parchment.
2. Wrap sausages with bacon rashers, cook properly for about 5 to 10 minutes in the oven, then turn and cook properly for about 5 to 10 more minutes. Separate yolks from white, add mustard and 1 teaspoon lemon juice, whisk with electrical blender on low speed; then pour olive and coconut oil little by little whisking constantly. Add the remaining lemon juice, salt and pepper, whisk thoroughly. Spread the remaining mustard over wrapped sausages, return to the oven for about 10 to 15 more minutes. Finally, cool for about 5 to 10 minutes and serve with made mayonnaise sauce. Serve.

134. Pinnacle Summer Veggies Surprise

Preparation Time: 15 minutes
Cooking Time: 4 hours
Servings: 4
Ingredients:

- 1 cup cherry tomatoes, halved
- 1/2 cup balsamic vinegar
- 2 cups okra, sliced
- About 1 cup olive oil
- 2 and 1/2 cups zucchini, sliced
- 1 tablespoon thyme, chopped
- 2 cups yellow bell pepper, chopped
- 1 cup mushrooms, sliced
- 2.5 tablespoons basil, chopped
- 1 red onion, chopped

Directions:

1. In a large bowl, mix onion chunks with tomatoes, okra, zucchini, mushrooms, bell pepper, basil and thyme. Add oil and vinegar and toss to coat everything. Transfer to your pot, cover and cook on medium for about 2 to 3 hours. Stir frequently.
2. Finally divide between plates and serve as a side dish.

135. Perfect Berry Delicious Smoothie

Preparation Time: 15 minutes
Cooking Time: 0 minutes
Servings: 3
Ingredients:

- Drop vanilla essence
- 2 cups mixed frozen berries
- 10 ice cubes
- 210 ml coconut Water

Directions:
1. Blend together all ingredients in a blender until very smooth. Finally add a little coconut milk if you like the smoothie to be thick. Enjoy!

136. Dashing Mini Baked Sweet Potato

Preparation Time: 5 minutes
Cooking Time: 10 minutes
Servings: 4
Ingredients:

- Chopped chives – 4 teaspoons
- Olive oil – 1.5 teaspoon
- Salt – ½ teaspoon
- Water – 1 cup
- Sweet potatoes – 4

Directions:
1. Prick the sweet potatoes using a fork then rub them with oil. Put the potatoes in a pot full of water and cook them for about 25 minutes; alternatively, if you have it, add water into the potatoes then place in microwave and cook at high heat for about 10 to 15 minutes. Cool them slightly once cooked. Split the potatoes partially into half lengthwise then fluff using a fork.
2. Finally sprinkle with salt and top with chives.

137. Super Peach Granita Almondine

Preparation Time: 10 minutes
Cooking Time: 20 minutes
Servings: 2
Ingredients:

- 2 tbsps. slivered almonds
- 1 tsp real almond extract
- ¼ tsp ground ginger
- ½ tsp ground nutmeg
- 3 large peaches

Directions:
1. Peel, pit and chop the peaches coarsely. Place the peaches, nutmeg, almond extract, and ginger in a food processor and blend until smooth. Pour the mixture in a glass baking dish, cover with foil and put in the freezer for about 3.5 hours. Scrape with a fork every 30 to 35 minutes. Serve in individual dishes, cover with slivered almonds.

138. Delightful Morning scramble

Preparation Time: 5 minutes

Cooking Time: 20 minutes

Servings: 4

Ingredients:

- 3 sweet potatoes
- 1.5 tablespoon coconut oil
- 30g chopped spinach leaves
- 150g meat pork

Directions:

1. Make a few holes in the sweet potatoes and cook them diced in a microwave oven for about 2 to 5 minutes if you have it, or alternatively in a pot full of water for about 20 minutes. After, pre-heat a skillet over medium heat, add coconut oil and diced sweet potatoes.
2. Fry for about 2 to 5 minutes till they are slightly brown.
3. Dice meat pork and add to the skillet. Stir and cook on medium for about 10 minutes.
4. Finally add chopped spinach, stir and transfer to plates.

139. Fantastic Easy Eggs and Chorizo

Preparation Time: 10 to 20 minutes

Cooking Time: 6 hours and 10 to 15 minutes

Servings: 4 to 6

Ingredients:

- 1 yellow onion, chopped
- 2.5 tablespoons coconut oil
- 1-pound chorizo, casings removed
- 1 butternut squash, peeled
- 12 eggs
- 4 garlic cloves, minced
- 1.5 cup coconut milk

Directions:

1. Heat up a pan with half of the oil over medium high heat; add onion and garlic, stir and sauté for about 4 to 5 minutes. Add chorizo chopped, stir, cook properly for about 2 to 5 minutes more and take off heat.
2. In a bowl, mix eggs with coconut milk and stir well; then grease your pot with the rest of the oil and add butternut squash on the bottom. Add onions mix and spread as well.
3. Add eggs at the end, cover and cook properly on low for about 5 to 6 hours. Stir occasionally.
4. Finally leave aside to cool down, slice and serve. It may be delicious for breakfast.

140. Great Pineapple and Coconut milk Smoothie

Preparation Time: 15 minutes

Cooking Time: 0 minutes

Servings: 4

Ingredients:

- 1 cup coconut milk
- 1 cup pineapple, frozen

Directions:

1. First of all, combine all ingredients in a blender and blend on high speed until very smooth.
2. Pour the smoothie into a tall serving glass. Serve with garnish, if you wish.

141. Happy Spiralized Sweet Potatoes

Preparation Time: 5 minutes

Cooking Time: 10 minutes

Servings: 4

Ingredients:

- 1 ½ teaspoon dried oregano
- Salt and pepper to taste

- 2 cups chicken stock
- 3 tablespoons capers
- 6 cups spiralized sweet potatoes
- 3 pints grape tomatoes
- 24 pitted, chopped olives
- 2 ½ tablespoons tomato paste
- ¼ cup chopped fresh basil
- ¼ cup olive oil
- 6 minced garlic cloves
- ¼ cup chopped parsley

Directions:

1. Heat a pot over medium heat; then add oil and swirl to coat. Add oregano, garlic and red pepper then cook properly for about 2 to 5 minutes as you constantly stir. Add stock then allow to boil.
2. Add spiralized sweet potatoes, tomato paste, and the tomatoes then cook properly for about 2 to 5 minutes or until the potatoes soften
3. Finally remove from heat then add the remaining ingredients as you toss to combine.

142. Lucky Paleo Basil Avocado Chicken Salad

Preparation Time: 15 minutes
Cooking Time: 0 minutes
Servings: 3
Ingredients:
- ½ cup fresh basil leaves
- Salt and pepper to taste
- 2 small avocados, pits and peeled
- 2.5 tbsps. extra virgin olive oil
- 2 boneless, cooked chicken breasts

Directions:

1. Place the cooked shredded chicken in a medium sized mixing bowl. Place the basil, olive oil, chopped avocado, salt and pepper in a food processor and blend until smooth.
2. Pour the avocado and basil mixture into the mixing bowl with the shredded chicken and toss well to coat. Taste and add additional salt and pepper if desired.
3. Finally keep in the fridge until ready to serve.

143. Vintage Canned Tuna Ceviche

Preparation Time: 20 minutes
Cooking Time: 0 minutes
Servings: 2
Ingredients:
- Limes – 2
- Sliced avocado – 2
- Salt and pepper as needed
- Tabasco sauce – 3 drops
- Olive oil – 1.5 tsp.
- 7 oz. tuna packed in water, drained
- Jalapeno – 1, minced
- Seeded plum tomato – 1, diced
- Chopped cilantro – 2.5 tbsps.
- Minced red onion – 2 tbsps.

Directions:

1. First of all, in a bowl, combine olive oil, juice of 1 lime, a pinch of kosher salt and red onion.
2. Mix in the tabasco, jalapeno, tomato, drained tuna, and chopped cilantro. Taste and adjust seasoning, then cover and marinate in the refrigerator for minimum 20 to 25 minutes.
3. Finally, top with fresh sliced avocado and serve.

144. Best Chicken with Mushroom Sauce

Preparation Time: 15 minutes
Cooking Time: 20 minutes
Servings: 4
Ingredients:

- 4.5 teaspoons olive oil
- ¼ cup chopped parsley
- 3 cloves garlic minced
- Salt and pepper to taste
- 12 ounces sliced mushrooms
- 1 cup fat free chicken broth
- 8 chicken tenderloins

Directions:

1. Preheat oven to 200°F. Sprinkle the chicken with salt and pepper.
2. Slice garlic and mushrooms. Add olive oil to a large skillet and heat over medium heat.
3. Add chicken and cook properly for about 5 to 10 minutes per side; then transfer to the oven.
4. Next, please add a little more oil to the skillet and then cook garlic for a few seconds before adding the mushrooms. Sprinkle the mushrooms with salt and pepper and cook, stirring once in a while, for about 5 to 10 minutes, until golden. Meanwhile, chop the parsley. Pour in chicken broth and stir in parsley, at the same time removing any brown bits from the bottom. Cook until the broth is reduced in half. Serve the chicken topped with mushroom sauce.

145. Nostalgic Lemon Poppyseed Mini Muffins

Preparation Time: 10 minutes
Cooking Time: 20 minutes
Servings: 5
Ingredients:

- 1 teaspoon baking soda
- 1 tablespoon water
- ¼ teaspoon organic sweetener
- ¼ cup lemon juice, + 1 tablespoon
- 2 tablespoons poppy seeds
- ¼ teaspoon salt
- 3 eggs
- 1.5 tablespoon raw honey
- 1 large lemon, zested
- 1/2 cup coconut flour
- 2.5 tablespoons butter, melted

Directions:

1. Preheat oven to 350° F. Oil the mini muffin pan with coconut oil or use liners.
2. In a bowl, add the dry ingredients and mix. Then, quickly add the remaining ingredients except the water and then mix until batter is wet and well incorporated. Let the batter sit once becoming foamy and thick for about 2 to 5 minutes. Add the water and blend again.
3. Scoop the batter into the muffin pan and bake for about 10 to 15 minutes. Finally cool a rack, and then enjoy!

146. Reliable Sweet Potato and Kale Chicken Patties

Preparation Time: 10 minutes
Cooking Time: 30 minutes
Servings: 5
Ingredients:

- 2 tablespoons coconut flour
- ½ sweet potato, peeled, cubed
- 3 cups of leaves kale, chopped
- 1 egg
- 1-pound boneless chicken breasts
- 1 teaspoon sea salt

- 1 tablespoon rosemary, minced
- 1 garlic clove, minced
- 1.5 teaspoon paprika
- 2 green onions, chopped
- 1 teaspoon Dijon mustard

Directions:

1. Heat a medium or large skillet over medium heat with about 1 teaspoon coconut oil or maybe avocado oil (or even bacon grease) and add green onions and then cook until tender, about 2 to 7 minutes; then quickly add sweet potatoes and cook properly for about 2 to 5 more minutes, until barely tender. Add kale and cook until wilted, about 2 to 5 minutes. Set aside.
2. Add chicken to a food processor and process on pulse until ground.
3. Transfer meat to a large mixing bowl. Add salt, garlic, rosemary, paprika, Dijon mustard, egg, coconut flour, and sweet potato mix. Mix together with hands until well combined.
4. Cover with plastic wrap and then refrigerate for at least 4 hours or maybe even better overnight.
5. Next, quickly divide your chicken mixture into 6 to 7 even patties.
6. Coat a medium or large non-stick pan with coconut oil or maybe even better bacon grease to just coat the bottom (not a lot).
7. Finally add patties and cook properly until golden crust forms, about 5 to 10 minutes, then flip to the other side and cook until golden and cooked through. Enjoy.

147. Charming California Grilled Chicken with Vinaigrette Dressing

Preparation Time: 10 minutes
Cooking Time: 0 minutes
Servings: 4
Ingredients:

- Red butter lettuce – 6 cups
- Diced avocado – 1 cup
- Diced red onion – 2.5 tbsps.
- Diced mango – 1 cup
- Grilled chicken breast – 12 oozes

FOR THE VINAIGRETTE:

- White vinegar – 2 tbsps.
- Olive oil – 2.5 tbsps.
- Salt and pepper to taste

Directions:

1. In a bowl, whisk vinaigrette ingredients and set aside. Toss red onion, mango, chicken, and avocado together. Divide baby greens into 4 small dishes. Top with avocado-chicken mixture and drizzle half the dressing or top. Finally serve with the rest of the dressing.

148. Chipotle Jicama Hash

Preparation Time: 10 minutes
Cooking Time: 15 minutes
Servings: 2
Ingredients:

- 4 slices bacon, chopped
- 12 oozes jicama, peeled and diced
- 4 oozes purple onion, chopped
- ½ green bell pepper seeded
- 4 tbsps. Chipotle mayonnaise

Directions:

1. Using a skillet, brown the bacon on a high heat for about 5 minutes. Remove and place on a towel to drain the grease. Use the remaining grease to fry the onions and jicama until brown.
2. When ready, add the chopped bell pepper and cook the hash until tender. Transfer the hash onto two plates and serve each plate with 4 tablespoons of Chipotle mayonnaise. Enjoy!

149. Fried Queso Blanco

Preparation Time: 20 minutes
Cooking Time: 170 minutes
Servings: 4
Ingredients:

- 5 oozes queso Blanco
- 1 ½ tbsp olive oil
- 3 oozes cheese
- 2 oozes olives
- 1 pinch red pepper flakes

Directions:

1. Cube some cheese and freeze it for 1-2 hours. Pour the oil in a skillet and heat to boil over a medium temperature. Add the cheese cubes and heat till brown. Combine the cheese using a spatula and flatten. Cook the cheese on both sides, flipping regularly.
2. While flipping, fold the cheese into itself to form crispy layers. Use a spatula to roll it into a block. Remove it from the pan, cool, cut it into small cubes, and serve.

150. Spinach with Bacon and Shallots

Preparation Time: 10 minutes
Cooking Time: 30 minutes
Servings: 4
Ingredients:

- 16 oozes raw spinach
- ½ cup chopped white onion
- ½ cup chopped shallot
- ½ pound raw bacon slices
- 2 tbsps. butter

Directions:

1. Slice the bacon strips into small narrow pieces. In a skillet, heat the butter and add the chopped onion, shallots and bacon. Sauté for 15-20 minutes or until the onions start to caramelize and the bacon is cooked. Add the spinach and sauté on a medium heat. Stir frequently to ensure the leaves touch the skillet while cooking. Cover and steam for around 5 minutes, stir and continue until wilted. Serve!

151. Bread-Wrapped Chicken Skewers

Preparation Time: 5 minutes   **Cooking Time:** 8 minutes   **Servings:** 2
Ingredients:

- 5 chicken breasts
- 10 slices bread
- A glass of Seed Oil

Directions:

1. Take a pan and add oil on the bottom. Heat on high the oil for 2-3 minutes.
2. Cut the chopped chicken breasts into four pieces. Slice the bread in half. Wrap the bread over the meat and mix. Fry them for 4-5 minutes until browned. Serve immediately.

152. Roasted Brussels Sprouts and Bacon

Preparation Time: 20 minutes
Cooking Time: 45 minutes
Servings: 2
Ingredients:

- 24 oozes brussels sprouts
- ¼ cup fish sauce
- ¼ cup bacon grease
- 6 strips bacon
- Pepper to taste

Directions:

1. De-stem and quarter the brussels sprouts. Mix them with the bacon grease and fish sauce.
2. Slice the bacon into small strips and cook. Add the bacon and pepper to the sprouts. Spread onto a greased skillet and cook on high for 25 minutes. Stir every 5 minutes or so. Broil for a few more minutes and serve.

153. Hillbilly Cheese Surprise

Preparation Time: 15 minutes
Cooking Time: 40 minutes
Servings: 6
Ingredients:

- 4 cups broccoli florets
- ¼ cup ranch dressing
- ½ cup sharp cheese, shredded
- ¼ cup heavy whipping cream
- Salt and pepper to taste

Directions:

1. Preheat your oven to 375°F/190°C. In a bowl, combine all of the ingredients until the broccoli is well-covered. In a casserole dish, spread out the broccoli mixture.
2. Bake for 30 minutes. Take out of your oven and mix. If the florets are not tender, bake for another 5 minutes until tender. Serve!

154. Parmesan and Garlic Cauliflower

Preparation Time: 20 minutes
Cooking Time: 40 minutes
Servings: 4
Ingredients:

- 3/4 cup cauliflower florets
- 2 tbsps. butter
- 1 clove garlic, sliced thinly
- 2 tbsps. shredded parmesan
- 1 pinch of salt

Directions:

1. Preheat your oven to 350°F/175°C. On a low heat, melt the butter with the garlic in a small pot for 5-10 minutes. Strain the garlic in a sieve. Add it, the cauliflower, parmesan and salt in a baking dish. Bake for 20 minutes or until golden. Serve warm.

155. Jalapeño Guacamole

Preparation Time: 10 minutes   **Cooking Time:** 30 minutes   **Servings:** 4
Ingredients:

- 2 Hass avocados, ripe
- ¼ red onion
- 1 jalapeño

- 1 tbsp lime juice
- Sea salt

Directions:

1. Spoon the avocado innings into a bowl. Dice the jalapeño and onion. Mash the avocado to the desired consistency. Add in the onion, jalapeño and lime juice. Sprinkle with salt. Serve.

156. Green Beans and Almonds

Preparation Time: 10 minutes
Cooking Time: 15 minutes
Servings: 4
Ingredients:

- 1 lb green beans, trimmed
- 2 tbsps. butter
- ¼ cup sliced almonds
- 2 tsps. lemon pepper

Directions:

1. Steam the green beans for 8 minutes, until tender, then drain. On a medium heat, melt the butter in a skillet. Sauté the almonds until browned. Sprinkle with salt and pepper. Mix in the green beans. Serve.

157. Sugar Snap Bacon

Preparation Time: 5 minutes
Cooking Time: 10 minutes
Servings: 4
Ingredients:

- 3 cups sugar snap peas

- ½ tbsp lemon juice
- 2 tbsps. bacon fat
- 2 tsps. garlic
- ½ tsp red pepper flakes

Directions:

1. In a skillet, cook the bacon fat until it begins to smoke. Add the garlic and cook for 2 minutes.
2. Add the sugar peas and lemon juice. Cook for 2-3 minutes. Remove and sprinkle with red pepper flakes and lemon zest. Serve!

158. Flax Cheese Chips

Preparation Time: 15 minutes
Cooking Time: 20 minutes
Servings: 2

Ingredients:

- 1 ½ cup cheddar cheese
- 4 tbsps. ground flaxseed meal
- Seasonings of your choice

Directions:

1. Preheat your oven to 425°F/220°C.
2. Spoon 2 tablespoons of cheddar cheese into a mound, onto a non-stick pad. Spread out a pinch of flax seed on each chip. Season and bake for 10-15 minutes. Serve.

159. Country Style Chard

Preparation Time: 5 minutes
Cooking Time: 5 minutes
Servings: 2
Ingredients:

- 4 slices bacon, chopped
- 2 tbsps. butter
- 2 tbsps. fresh lemon juice

- ½ tsp garlic paste
- 1 bunch Swiss chard, chopped

Directions:

1. On a medium heat, cook the bacon in a skillet until the fat begins to brown. Melt the butter in the skillet and add the lemon juice and garlic paste. Add the chard leaves and cook until they begin to wilt. Cover and turn up the heat to high. Cook for 3 minutes.
2. Mix well, sprinkle with salt and serve.

160. Kale Crisps

Preparation Time: 5 minutes
Cooking Time: 15 minutes
Servings: 1
Ingredients:

- 1 large bunch kale
- 2 tbsps. olive oil
- 1 tbsp seasoned salt

Directions:

1. Preheat your oven to 350°F/175°C.
2. De-stem, wash and dry the kale. Put it inside a cooking-zip loc bag and shake with oil. Put the kale on a baking sheet. Bake for 10 minutes. Remove and serve hot!

161. Baked Tortillas

Preparation Time: 10 minutes
Cooking Time: 30 minutes
Servings: 4
Ingredients:

- 1 large head of cauliflower
- 4 large eggs
- 2 garlic cloves, minced
- 1 ½ tsp thyme
- ½ tsp salt

Directions:

1. Preheat your oven to 375°F/190°C. Put parchment paper on two baking sheets.
2. In a food processor, break down the cauliflower into rice.
3. Add ¼ cup water and the riced cauliflower to a saucepan. Cook on a medium high heat until tender for 10 minutes. Drain. Mix the cauliflower, eggs, garlic, thyme and salt.
4. Make 4 thin circles on the parchment paper. Bake for 20 minutes, until dry. Serve warm.

162. Spinach Artichoke-stuffed Chicken Breasts

Preparation Time: 15 Minutes
Cooking Time: 15 Minutes
Servings: 6
Ingredients:

- ¼ cup Greek yogurt
- ¼ cup spinach, drained
- ½ cup artichoke hearts, sliced
- ½ cup mozzarella cheese
- 1 ½ lb. chicken breasts
- 2 tbsps. olive oil
- 4 oozes cream cheese
- Sea salt and pepper, to taste

Directions:

1. Pound the chicken breasts to a thickness of about one inch. Using a sharp knife, slice a "pocket" into the side of each. This is where you will put the filling. Sprinkle the breasts with salt and pepper and set aside.
2. In a medium bowl, combine cream cheese, yogurt, mozzarella, spinach, artichoke, salt, and pepper and mix thoroughly. A hand mixer may be the easiest way to combine all the ingredients thoroughly. Spoon the mixture into each breast's pockets and set aside while you heat a large skillet over medium heat and warm the oil in it. If you have an extra filling you can't fit into the breasts, set it aside until just before your chicken is done cooking.
3. Cook each breast for about eight minutes per side, then pull off the heat when it reaches an internal temperature of about 165° Fahrenheit. Before you pull the chicken out of the pan, heat the remaining filling to warm it through and rid it of any cross-contamination from the chicken. Once hot, top the chicken breasts with it. Serve!

163. Chicken Parmesan

Preparation Time: 20 Minutes
Cooking Time: 15 Minutes
Servings: 4
Ingredients:
- ¼ cup of avocado oil
- ¼ cup of almond flour
- ¼ cup parmesan cheese
- ¾ cup of marinara sauce, sugar-free
- ¾ cup mozzarella cheese, shredded
- 2 eggs, beaten
- 2 tsps. Italian seasoning
- 3 oozes pork rinds, pulverized
- 4 lbs. chicken breasts, boneless
- Sea salt and pepper, to taste

Directions:
1. Preheat the oven to 450° F and grease a baking dish.
2. Place the beaten egg into one shallow dish. Place the almond flour in another. In a third dish, combine the pork rinds, parmesan, and Italian seasoning and mix well. Pat the chicken breasts dry and pound them down to about ½" thick. Dredge the chicken in the almond flour, then coat in egg, then coat in crumb. Heat a large sauté pan over medium-high heat and warm oil until shimmering. Once the oil is hot, lay the breasts into the pan and not move them until they've had a chance to cook. Cook for about two minutes, then flip as gently as possible (a fish spatula is perfect) then cook for two more. Remove the pan from the heat.
3. Place the breasts in the greased baking dish and top with marinara sauce and mozzarella cheese. Bake for about 10 minutes. Serve warm.

164. Sheet Pan Jalapeño Burgers

Preparation Time: 10 Minutes
Cooking Time: 20 Minutes
Servings: 4
Ingredients:
- 24 oozes ground beef
- Sea salt and pepper, to taste
- ½ tsp. garlic powder
- 6 slices bacon, halved

- 1 med. onion, sliced
- 2 jalapeños, seeded and sliced
- 4 slices pepper jack cheese
- ¼ cup of mayonnaise
- 1 tbsp. chili sauce
- ½ tsp. Worcestershire sauce
- 8 lbs. leaves of butter lettuce
- 8 dill pickle chips

Directions:

1. Preheat the oven to 425° F and line a baking sheet with non-stick foil. Mix the salt, pepper, and garlic into the ground beef and form 4 patties out of it. Line the burgers, bacon slices, jalapeño slices, and onion rounds onto the baking sheet and bake for about 18 minutes.
2. Top each patty with a piece of cheese and set the oven to boil. Broil for 2 minutes, then remove the pan from the oven. Serve one patty with 3 pieces of bacon, jalapeño slices, onion rounds, and desired amount of sauce with 2 pickle chips and 2 parts of lettuce. Enjoy!

165. Grilled Herb Garlic Chicken

Preparation Time: 5 Minutes
Cooking Time: 10 Minutes
Servings: 2
Ingredients:

- 1 ¼ lb. chicken breasts

- 1 tbsp. garlic and
- 1 tbsp. herb seasoning mix
- 2 tsps. extra virgin olive oil
- Sea salt and pepper, to taste

Directions:

1. Heat a grill pan or your grill. Coat the chicken breasts in a little bit of olive oil and then sprinkle the seasoning mixture onto them, rubbing it in.
2. Cook the chicken for about eight minutes per side and make sure the chicken has reached an internal temperature of 165° F. Serve hot with your favorite sides!

166. Blackened Salmon with Avocado Salsa

Preparation Time: 30 Minutes
Cooking Time: 21 Minutes
Servings: 6
Ingredients:

- 1 tbsp. extra virgin olive oil
- 4 filets of salmon
- 4 tsps. Cajun seasoning

- 2 med. avocados, diced
- 1 cup cucumber, diced
- ¼ cup red onion, diced
- 1 tbsp. parsley, chopped
- 1 tbsp. lime juice
- Salt and pepper, to taste

Directions:

1. Heat a skillet over medium-high heat and warm the oil in it. Rub the Cajun seasoning into the fillets, then lay them into the skillet's bottom once it's hot enough. Cook until a dark crust forms, then flip and repeat. In a medium mixing bowl, combine all the ingredients for the salsa and set aside. Plate the fillets and top with ¼ of the salsa yielded. Enjoy!

167. Delectable Tomato Slices

Preparation Time: 15 Minutes

Cooking Time: 15 Minutes

Servings: 10

Ingredients:

- ½ cup of. mayonnaise
- ½ cup of. ricotta cheese, shredded
- ½ cup part-skim mozzarella cheese
- ½ cup of parmesan, grated
- 1 tsp. garlic, minced
- 1 tbsp. dried oregano, crushed
- Salt, to taste
- 4 large tomatoes, cut in slices

Directions:

1. Preheat the oven to broiler on high. Arrange a rack about 3-inch from the heating element.
2. In a bowl, add the mayonnaise, cheeses, garlic, oregano, and salt and mix until well combined and smooth. Spread the cheese mixture over each tomato slice evenly. Arrange the tomato slices onto a broiler pan in a single layer. Broil for about 3-5 minutes or until the top becomes golden brown. Remove from the oven and transfer the tomato slices onto a platter. Set aside to cool slightly. Serve warm.

168. Grain-free Tortilla Chips

Preparation Time: 15 Minutes

Cooking Time: 16 Minutes

Servings: 6

Ingredients:

- 1½ cup mozzarella cheese
- ½ cup of almond flour
- 1 tbsp. golden flaxseed meal
- Salt and pepper, to taste

Directions:

1. Preheat the oven to 375° F. Line 2 large baking sheets with parchment paper.
2. In a microwave-safe bowl, add the cheese and microwave for about 1 minute, stirring after every 15 seconds. In the bowl of melted cheese, add the almond flour, flaxseed meal, salt, and black pepper and with a fork, mix well. With your hands, knead until a dough form. Make 2 equal sized balls from the dough. Place 1 dough ball onto each prepared baking sheet and roll into an 8x10-inch rectangle. Cut each dough rectangle into triangle-shaped chips. Arrange the chips in a single layer. Bake for about 10-15 minutes, flipping once halfway through.
3. Remove from oven and set aside to cool before serving.

Strong Paleo Soups, Stews and Chilies

169. Chicken Turnip Soup

Preparation Time: 10 minutes
Cooking Time: 6 to 8 hours
Servings: 5
Ingredients:

- 340g bone-in chicken
- ¼ cup turnip, chopped

- ¼ cup onions, chopped
- 4 garlic cloves, smashed
- 4 cups water
- 3 sprigs thyme
- 2 bay leaves
- Salt, and pepper to taste

Directions:

1. Put the chicken, turnip, onions, garlic, water, thyme springs, and bay leaves in a pot. Season with salt and pepper, then give the mixture a good stir. Cover and cook on low for 6 to 8 hours until the chicken is cooked through. Stir frequently. When ready, remove the bay leaves and shred the chicken with a fork. Divide the soup among five bowls and serve.

170. Brown Rice Mushrooms Vegetarian Stew

Servings: 6
Cooking Time: 4 hours
Ingredients

- 2 chopped onions
- 2 tablespoons olive oil
- 1 sprig thyme, minced

- 4 chopped carrots
- 1 cup brown rice
- 2 cups mushrooms, sliced
- 4 cups chicken stock
- Salt and pepper to taste
- 1 bunch chopped parsley

Instructions

1. Put all ingredients in the slow cooker and cook on low for 4 hours.

171. Black Bean, Chicken & Brown Rice Stew

Servings: 8
Cooking Time: 4 hours
Ingredients

- 1 cup brown rice
- 1 chopped onion
- 2 tablespoons olive oil

- 1 cup uncooked black beans
- Salt, and pepper
- 1 teaspoon ground cumin
- 4 cups chicken stock
- 4 pounds chicken breast, chopped

Instructions

1. Put ingredients in the pot. Cover, and cook on low for 4 hours.

172. Pork White Bean Chili

Servings: 8
Cooking Time: 4 hours
Ingredients

- 2 red peppers, sliced
- 2 chopped onions
- 2 tablespoons olive oil
- 1 cup uncooked white beans

- 1/2 sliced jalapeno peppers
- 1 cup sweet corn
- Salt and pepper
- 2 teaspoons ground cumin
- 3 cups beef stock
- 4 pounds chopped pork meat

Instructions

1.Put ingredients in the pot. Cover, and cook on low for 4 hours.

173. Pork Meat Stew

Servings: 8
Cooking Time: 3 hours 30 minutes
Ingredients

- 3 large tomatoes, sliced
- 1 chopped onion
- 2 tablespoons olive oil

- 2 large red peppers, sliced
- 1 bunch chopped parsley
- Salt and pepper
- 2 teaspoons ground cumin
- 1 cup beef stock
- 4 pounds cubed pork meat

Instructions

Put ingredients in the pot. Cover, and cook on low for 3 hours 30 minutes.

174. Lamb & Zucchini Stew

Servings: 8
Cooking Time: 3 hours
Ingredients

- 2 medium zucchinis, sliced
- 1 cup chopped onions
- 2 tablespoons olive oil
- 2 sliced tomatoes

- 2 yellow peppers, sliced
- 2 sprigs rosemary, minced
- Salt and pepper
- 1 teaspoon cumin
- 1 cup beef stock
- 4 pounds cubed lamb meat

Instructions

Put ingredients in the one pot. Cover, and cook on low for 3 hours.

175. Chicken, Garlic & Tomato Stew

Servings: 8
Cooking Time: 2 hours 30 minutes.
Ingredients

- 3 tomatoes, chopped
- 2 chopped onions
- 2 tablespoons olive oil

- 1 garlic bulb, cutted
- Salt and pepper
- 2 teaspoons cumin
- 1 garlic clove
- 4 pounds chicken breast, chopped

Instructions

1.Put ingredients in the pot. Cover, and cook on low for 2 hours 30 minutes.

176. Chicken & Onion Stew

Servings: 8
Cooking Time: 4 hours
Ingredients

- 1 cup sliced mushrooms
- 6 large onions, chopped

- 2 tablespoons olive oil
- Salt and pepper to taste
- 2 cups chicken stock
- 4 pounds chicken breast

Instructions

1.Put ingredients in the pot. Cover, and cook on low for 4 hours.

177. Pork Stew with Plums

Servings: 6

Cooking Time: 6 hours

Ingredients

- 1 cup chopped onions
- 2 tablespoons olive oil
- 3 pounds chopped pork meat
- 2 chopped carrots
- 1 1/2 cup chicken stock
- 1/2 cup red wine
- Salt and pepper to taste
- 2 cups halved ripe plums, stoned
- 2 garlic cloves

Instructions

1. Add all ingredients to pot and cover with the lid. Cook on low for 6 hours.

178. Chicken Mushrooms & Olives Stew

Servings: 6
Cooking Time: 6 hours
Ingredients

- 4 pounds chicken with skin on
- 3 large chopped carrots
- 1 chopped onion
- 2 tablespoons olive oil
- 1 cup sliced mushrooms
- 1/2 cup chopped celery
- 1 cup black olives
- Salt and pepper to taste
- 1 garlic clove, minced
- ½ cup fresh parsley

Instructions

1. Put all ingredients in the crockpot, cover and cook on low 6 hours.

179. Pork, Celery and Basil Stew

Servings: 8
Cooking Time: 8 hours
Ingredients

- 1 chopped onion
- 2 Tablespoons coconut oil
- 3 pounds chopped pork meat
- 3 chopped carrots
- 2 1/2 cups beef stock
- 1 cup red wine
- Salt and pepper to taste
- 1 bunch chopped parsley
- 1 cup chopped celery
- 1/2 cup fresh basil

Instructions

1. Add all ingredients to slow cooker and cook on low for 8 hours.

180. Irish Stew

Servings: 8
Cooking Time: 5 hours
Ingredients

- 2 chopped onions
- 3 tablespoons olive oil
- 1 sprig thyme
- 3 pounds chopped lamb meat
- 4 chopped carrots
- 1/2 cup brown rice
- 6 cups chicken stock
- Salt and pepper to taste
- 1 tablespoon minced parsley
- 1 tablespoon minced bay leaf
- 3 chopped sweet potatoes
- 1 bunch chopped parsley
- 1 bunch chives

Instructions

1. Put all ingredients in the slow cooker and cook on low for 6 hours.

181. Hungarian Pea Stew

Servings: 8
Cooking Time: 6 hours
Ingredients

- 6 cups green peas
- 1-pound cubed pork
- 3 tablespoons olive oil

- 4 tablespoons almond flour
- 2 tablespoons minced parsley
- 1 cup water
- Salt to taste
- 1 cup coconut milk
- 1 teaspoon coconut sugar

Instructions

1.Put all ingredients in the slow cooker and cook on low for 6 hours.

182. A Simple Age-Old Bone Broth

Preparation Time: 10 minutes
Cooking Time: 75 minutes
Servings: 2
Ingredients:

- 1 cooked chicken carcass

- inch knob of ginger
- 1 chopped sized onion
- 1 cup of chopped up celery tops
- 2 tablespoon of apple cider vinegar
- 3 liters of water

Directions:

1. Add all of the listed ingredients to your pot. Pour 3 liters of water into the pot; cover and cook it for about 75 minutes on low heat. Stir frequently. Once done, turn off the heat, but don't remove the lid to release heat naturally. Allow it to cool down for about 1 hour.
2. Strain the solids into a large sized container and season the broth with some salt. Allow it to chill overnight. The day after, remove the solidified fat from the top. Divide it and enjoy!

183. Lamb and Vegetable Stew

Servings: 6
Cooking Time: 6 hours
Ingredients

- 2 pounds Lamb stew meat
- 2 chopped Tomatoes
- 1 Summer squash
- 1 Zucchini
- 1 cup Mushrooms, sliced

- 1/2 Bell peppers, chopped
- 1 Onions, chopped
- Salt
- 1 garlic clove, crushed
- 1/2 teaspoon Thyme leaves
- 4 Bay leaves
- 2 cups chicken broth

Instructions

1.Cut squash and zucchini. Place vegetables and lamb in crockpot. Mix salt, garlic, thyme, and bay leaf into broth and pour over lamb and vegetables. Cover and cook on low for 6 hours. Serve over brown rice.

184. Zucchini, Tomato & Pork Stew

Servings: 8
Cooking Time: 3 hours
Ingredients

- 2 cups cooked corn
- 1 chopped onion
- 2 sliced zucchinis

- 2 chopped tomato
- 2 tablespoon olive oil
- 2 garlic cloves
- Salt and pepper
- 4 pounds cubed pork

Instructions

1.Put ingredients in the pot. Cover, and cook on low for 3 hours.

185. Spinach Mushroom Soup

Preparation Time: 10 minutes
Cooking Time: 5 minutes
Servings: 3
Ingredients:
- 1 tablespoon olive oil
- 1 teaspoon garlic, chopped
- 1 cup spinach, torn
- ½ cup mushrooms, chopped
- Salt and pepper, to taste
- ½ teaspoon tamari
- 3 cups vegetable stock
- 1 teaspoon sesame seeds, roasted

Directions:
1. Heat on medium the olive oil in a skillet. Add garlic to the hot oil and sauté for 30 seconds or until fragrant. Add spinach and mushrooms, then sauté for 1 minute or until lightly tender.
2. Add salt, black pepper, tamari, and vegetable stock. Cook for another 3 minutes. Stir constantly.
3. Garnish with sesame seeds and serve warm.

186. Garlicky Chicken Soup

Preparation Time:10 minutes
Cooking Time: 10 minutes
Servings: 4
Ingredients:
- 2 tablespoons butter
- 1 large chicken breast chopped
- 4 ounces cream cheese, cubed
- 2 tablespoons garlic powder
- ½ cup heavy cream
- 14½ ounces chicken broth
- Salt, to taste

Directions:
1. Place a skillet and add butter to melt on medium heat. Add chicken strips and sauté for 2 minutes. Add cream cheese and garlic powder, and cook for 3 minutes, stirring occasionally.
2. Pour in the heavy cream and chicken broth. Bring the soup to a boil, then lower the heat. Simmer the soup for 4 minutes, then sprinkle with salt. Let cool for 5 minutes and serve warm.

187. Lamb and Sweet Potato Stew

Servings: 8
Cooking Time: 6 hours
Ingredients
- 1 cup tomato paste
- 1/4 cup lemon juice
- 2 tablespoons mustard
- Salt and pepper to taste
- 1/2 cup soft almond butter
- 3 cubed sweet potatoes
- 1/2 garlic clove minced
- 4 pounds boneless chuck roast

Instructions

1.In a large bowl, combine tomato paste, lemon juice, almond butter and mustard. Stir in salt, pepper, garlic and cubed sweet potato. Place chuck roast in a slow cooker. Pour tomato mixture over chuck roast. Cover, and cook on low for 6 hours.

188. Cauliflower Curry Soup

Preparation Time: 15 minutes
Cooking Time: 26 minutes
Servings: 4
Ingredients:

74

- 2 tablespoons avocado oil
- 1 white onion, chopped
- 4 garlic cloves, chopped
- ½ Serrano pepper, chopped
- inch ginger, chopped
- ¼ teaspoon turmeric powder
- 2 teaspoons curry powder
- ½ teaspoon black pepper
- 1 teaspoon salt
- 1 cup of water
- 1 large cauliflower, cut into florets
- 1 cup chicken broth
- 1 can unsweetened coconut milk
- Cilantro, for garnish

Directions:

1. Place a saucepan over medium heat and add oil to heat. Add onions to the hot oil and sauté them for 3 minutes. Add garlic, Serrano pepper, and ginger, then sauté for 2 minutes.
2. Add turmeric, curry powder, black pepper, and salt. Cook for 1 minute after a gentle stir.
3. Pour water into the pan, then add cauliflower. Cover this soup with a lid and cook for 10 minutes. Stir constantly. Remove the soup from the heat and allow it to cool at room temperature. Transfer this soup to a blender and purée the soup until smooth.
4. Return the soup to the saucepan and add broth and coconut milk. Cook for 10 minutes more and stir frequently.
5. Divide the soup into four bowls and sprinkle the cilantro on top for garnish before serving.

189. Asparagus Cream Soup

Preparation Time: 15 minutes
Cooking Time: 22 minutes
Servings: 6
Ingredients:

- 4 tablespoons butter
- 1 small onion, chopped
- 6 cups low-sodium chicken broth
- Salt and pepper, to taste
- 2 pounds asparagus, cut in half
- ½ cup sour cream

Directions:

1. Place a large pot over low heat and add butter to melt. Add onion to the melted butter and sauté for 2 minutes or until soft. Add chicken broth, salt, black pepper, and asparagus. Bring the soup to a boil, then cover the lid and cook for 20 minutes. Remove the pot from the heat and allow it to cool for 5 minutes. Transfer the soup to a blender and blend until smooth. Add sour cream and pulse again to mix well. Serve fresh and warm.

190. Red Gazpacho Cream Soup

Preparation Time: 15 minutes
Cooking Time: 20 minutes
Servings: 10
Ingredients:

- 1 large red bell pepper, halved
- 1 large green bell pepper, halved
- 2 tablespoons basil, chopped
- 4 medium tomatoes
- 1 small red onion
- 1 large cucumber, diced
- 2 medium spring onions, diced
- 2 tablespoons apple cider vinegar
- 2 garlic cloves
- 2 tablespoons fresh lemon juice
- 1 cup extra virgin olive oil
- Salt and pepper, to taste
- 1¼ pounds feta cheese, shredded

Directions:

1. Preheat the oven to 400°F (205°C) and line a baking tray with parchment paper.

2. Place all the bell peppers in the baking tray and roast in the preheated oven for 20 minutes.
3. Remove the bell peppers from the oven. Allow to cool, then peel off their skin.
4. Transfer the peeled bell peppers to a blender along with basil, tomatoes, red onions, cucumber, spring onions, vinegar, garlic, lemon juice, olive oil, black pepper, and salt. Blend until the mixture smooth. Add black pepper and salt to taste. Garnish with feta cheese and serve warm.

191. Beef Taco Soup

Preparation Time: 15 minutes
Cooking Time: 24 minutes
Servings: 8
Ingredients:
- 2 garlic cloves, minced
- ½ cup onions, chopped
- pound (454 g) ground beef

- 1 teaspoon chili powder
- 1 tablespoon ground cumin
- 8-ounce cream cheese, softened
- 10-ounce diced tomatoes and green chilies
- ½ cup heavy cream
- 2 teaspoons salt
- 14½-ounce beef broth

Directions:
1. Take a large saucepan and place it over medium-high heat.
2. Add garlic, onions, and ground beef to the soup and sauté for 7 minutes until meat is browned.
3. Add chili powder and cumin, then cook for 2 minutes.
4. Add cream cheese and cook for 5 minutes while mashing the cream cheese into the beef with a spoon. Add diced tomatoes and green chilies, heavy cream, salt and broth then cook for 10 minutes. Mix gently and serve warm.

192. Creamy Tomato Soup

Preparation Time: 15 minutes
Cooking Time: 30 minutes
Servings: 4
Ingredients:
- 2 cups of water
- 4 cups tomato juice

- 3 tomatoes, peeled, seeded and diced
- 14 leaves fresh basil
- 2 tablespoons butter
- 1 cup heavy whipping cream
- Salt and pepper, to taste

Directions:
1. Take a suitable pot and place it over medium heat. Add water, tomato juice, and tomatoes, then simmer for 30 minutes. Transfer the soup to a blender, then add basil leaves. Blend the soup until smooth. Return this tomato soup to the cooking pot and place it over medium heat. Add butter, heavy cream, salt, and black pepper. Cook and mix until the butter melts.
2. Serve warm and fresh.

193. Okra and Beef Stew

Preparation Time: 15 minutes
Cooking Time: 3 hours
Servings: 3
Ingredients:
- 6 oz okra, chopped
- 8 oz beef sirloin, chopped

- 1 cup of water
- ¼ cup coconut cream
- 1 teaspoon dried basil
- ¼ teaspoon cumin seeds
- 1 tablespoon avocado oil

Directions:

1. Add all ingredients to the pot and cook for 3 hours. Serve warm.

194. Chipotle Stew

Preparation Time: 15 minutes
Cooking Time: 2 hours 30 minutes
Servings: 3
Ingredients:

- 2 chipotle chili, chopped
- 1 oz fresh cilantro, chopped
- 9 oz chicken fillet, chopped
- 1 teaspoon ground paprika
- 2 tablespoons sesame seeds
- ¼ teaspoon salt
- 1 cup chicken broth

Directions:

1. Add all ingredients to the pot and cook for 2 hours and 30 minutes. Serve warm.

195. Lamb Soup

Preparation Time: 10 minutes
Cooking Time: 4 hours
Servings: 4
Ingredients:

- ½ cup broccoli, chopped
- 7 oz lamb fillet, chopped
- ¼ teaspoon ground cumin
- ¼ daikon, chopped
- 2 bell peppers, chopped
- 1 tablespoon avocado oil
- 5 cups beef broth

Directions:

1. Add all ingredients to the pot and cook for 4 hours. Serve warm.

196. Basic Minestrone Soup

Preparation Time: 10 minutes
Cooking Time: 2 hours 30 minutes
Servings: 4
Ingredients:

- 1 ½ cup ground pork
- ½ bell pepper, chopped
- 2 tablespoons chives, chopped
- 2 oz celery stalk, chopped
- 1 teaspoon butter
- 1 teaspoon Italian seasonings
- 4 cups chicken broth
- ½ cup mushrooms, sliced

Directions:

1. Add all ingredients to the pot and cook for 2 hours 30 minutes. Serve warm.

197. Chorizo Soup

Preparation Time: 10 minutes
Cooking Time: 3 hours
Servings: 3 servings
Ingredients:

- 8 oz chorizo, chopped
- 1 teaspoon tomato paste
- 4 oz scallions, diced
- 1 tablespoon dried cilantro
- ½ teaspoon chili powder
- 1 teaspoon avocado oil
- 2 cups beef broth

Directions:

1. Add all ingredients to the pot and cook for 3 hours. Serve warm.

198. Red Feta Soup

Preparation Time: 10 minutes
Cooking Time: 1 hour 30 minutes
Servings: 4

Ingredients:

- 1 cup broccoli, chopped

- 1 teaspoon tomato paste
- ½ cup coconut cream
- 4 cups beef broth
- 1 teaspoon chili flakes
- 6 oz feta, crumbled

Directions:
1. Add all ingredients to the pot and cook for 1 hour 30 minutes. Serve warm.

199. "Ramen" Soup

Preparation Time: 10 minutes
Cooking Time: 1 hour 30 minutes
Servings: 2
Ingredients:
- 1 zucchini, trimmed
- 2 cups chicken broth
- 2 eggs, boiled, peeled
- 1 tablespoon coconut aminos
- 5 oz beef loin, strips
- 1 teaspoon chili flakes
- 1 tablespoon chives, chopped
- ½ teaspoon salt

Directions:
1. Add all ingredients to the pot and cook for 1 hour 30 minutes. Serve warm.

200. Tomatillos Fish Stew

Preparation Time: 15 minutes
Cooking Time: 1 hour 30 minutes
Servings: 2
Ingredients:
- 2 tomatillos, chopped
- 10 oz salmon fillet, chopped
- 1 teaspoon ground paprika
- ½ teaspoon ground turmeric
- 1 cup coconut cream
- ½ teaspoon salt

Directions:
1. Add all ingredients to the pot and cook for 1 hour 30 minutes. Serve warm.

201. Chili Verde Soup

Preparation Time: 10 minutes
Cooking Time: 2 hours
Servings: 4
Ingredients:
- 2 oz chili Verde sauce
- ½ cup Cheddar cheese, shredded
- 5 cups chicken broth
- 2 pounds chicken breast, boneless
- 1 tablespoon dried cilantro

Directions:
1. Add all ingredients to the pot and cook for 2 hours. Serve warm.

202. Steak Soup

Preparation Time: 10 minutes
Cooking Time: 4 hours
Servings: 5
Ingredients:
- 5 oz scallions, diced
- 1 tablespoon coconut oil
- 1 oz daikon, diced
- pound beef round steak, chopped
- 1 teaspoon dried thyme
- 5 cups of water
- ½ teaspoon ground black pepper

Directions:
1. Add all ingredients to the pot and cook for 4 hours. Serve warm.

203. Meat Spinach Stew

Preparation Time: 20 minutes
Cooking Time: 2 hours
Servings: 4
Ingredients:

- 2 cups spinach, chopped
- pound beef sirloin, chopped
- 1 teaspoon allspices
- 3 cups chicken broth
- 1 cup of coconut milk
- 1 teaspoon coconut aminos

Directions:

1. Add all ingredients to the pot and cook for 2 hours. Serve warm.

Delicious Salad Recipes

204. Green Grain Bowl

Preparation Time: 10 minutes   **Cooking Time:** 55 minutes   **Servings:** 4

Ingredients:

- Broccoli – 2 cups
- Diced carrots – 1 cup
- Diced onion – ½ cup
- Garbanzo beans – 1 can
- Salt – ½ teaspoon
- Olive oil – 2 tablespoons
- Rosemary – 1 teaspoon
- Pepper – ½ teaspoon
- Quinoa – 2 cups dried
- Non-stick cooking spray
- 4 eggs (fried)
- Greek yogurt – 2 tablespoons

Directions:

1. Preheat the oven to a temperature of 400°F. Place a foil over the baking sheet, and put the broccoli, onion, garbanzo beans and carrots on it. Then pour over it 2 tablespoons of olive oil. Toss this mixture, and season with pepper, salt, rosemary and toss. Put in the oven and bake for about 20 minutes or alternatively, till the broccoli begins to turn golden brown.
2. Put 4 cups of water and 2 cups of quinoa into a medium-sized pot and heat this mixture until it becomes to boil. Then lower the heat and leave covered for 10 – 12 minutes or alternatively, till the water had been completely absorbed. Allow to cool. Spray your pan with the cooking spray, and place over medium heat. Break each egg at a time and pour into the pan. Allow the egg to cook for about 2 minutes. Add pepper and salt for seasoning, then flip and allow the other side to cook for about 2 minutes. To serve, place 1 cup of cooked quinoa, 1 fried egg and 1 cup of roasted vegetables in each bowl. Then top with Greek yogurt, as desired. Serve!

205. Salad Grain Bowl

Preparation Time: 10 minutes
Cooking Time: 35 minutes
Servings: 1

Ingredients:

- Baby spinach – two handfuls
- 1 boiled egg
- Cooked brown rice – ¼ cup
- Grape tomatoes – 6
- Avocado – ½
- Garbanzo beans – ¼ cup
- Goat cheese – 1
- Olive oil – ½ tablespoon
- Balsamic vinegar – ½ tablespoon
- Pepper and salt, for seasoning

Directions:

1. First of all, rinse the tomatoes, garbanzo beans and spinach with clean water and pat dry. Peel the egg; the and slice it and the avocado. Measure out a portion of the rice, goat cheese and garbanzo beans. Next step is the preparation of balsamic vinaigrette: put the ½ tablespoon of balsamic vinegar, ½ tablespoon of olive oil, pepper and salt in a small bowl and whisk thoroughly. Place two handfuls of baby spinach in a large salad bowl, arrange the rest of the salad on top and pour the dressing. Enjoy!

206. Cucumber and Tomato Salad

Preparation Time: 5 minutes   **Servings:** 6
Cooking Time: 0 minutes   **Ingredients:**

- 1 Cucumber – peeled, sliced
- 3 tomatoes – seeded, chopped
- 1/3 cup of oregano – chopped
- Olive oil – 1 tablespoon
- Salt and pepper

Directions:
1. In a medium-sized bowl, combine the ingredients. Toss the ingredients and mix properly. Serve!

207. Avocado and Chicken Egg Salad Sandwich

Preparation Time: 10 minutes
Cooking Time: 0 minutes.
Servings: 6
Ingredients:
- 2 eggs – hard-boiled, chopped
- 2 egg whites – hard-boiled, chopped
- 1 shredded chicken breast – cooked
- 2 avocados – small, peeled
- Greek yogurt – 1 tablespoon
- Green onion – 2 tablespoons
- Lemon juice – 1 tablespoon
- Dijon mustard – ¼ tablespoon
- Salt and pepper

Directions:
1. Put the eggs, chicken, avocados, egg whites, Greek yogurt, green onion, lemon juice and mustard in a bowl. Mash the combination with a fork and add salt and pepper to taste. Enjoy!

208. Tuna Apple Salad

Preparation Time: 15 minutes
Cooking Time: 0 minutes
Servings: 6
Ingredients:
- Water-packed tuna – 6 ounces
- 1 Medium apple (chopped)
- Red onion (chopped) – 2 tablespoons
- Celery (chopped) – ¼ cup
- Golden raisins – ¼ cup
- Salad greens – 2 cups
- Italian dressing – 3 tablespoons
- Whole wheat pita – 2

Directions:
1. Place tuna, apple, onion and raisins in a small bowl. Add 2 tablespoons of dressing and stir. Toss salad greens with 1 tablespoon of dressing in a medium-sized bowl. Cut pitas into two and fill each with equal amounts of tuna salad and salad greens. Enjoy!

209. Chicken Tomatillo Salad

Preparation Time: 10 minutes
Cooking Time: 20minutes
Servings: 5
Ingredients:
FOR SALAD:
- Cooked chicken (chopped) – 2 cups
- Frozen corn (thawed) – 1 cup
- Red bell pepper (chopped) – 1 cup
- Carrots (chopped) – 1 cup
- Green onions (sliced) – 4
- Fresh cilantro (chopped) – ¼ cup

FOR DRESSING:
- Tomatillos (husked, quartered) – 1 cup
- Anaheim chili (seeded, chopped) – 1
- Italian dressing – 3 tablespoons
- Black pepper (ground) – ½ teaspoon

Directions:
1. Put tomatillos, Italian dressing, ground pepper and Anaheim salad in a blender and mash. Combine chopped chicken, thawed frozen corn, chopped carrots, sliced green onions, chopped bell pepper

and chopped cilantro in a bowl and toss. Place the dressing over the salad and toss very well. Toss until it coats, then cover and store in a fridge. You can serve it the next day with lettuce on its side.

210. Strawberry Mint Salad

Preparation Time: 2 to 5 minutes
Cooking Time: 5 to 10 minutes
Servings: 1 to 2
Ingredients:

- Fresh lemon juice – about 1.5 tablespoon
- Skinned and chopped cucumber – 2 cups
- Pinch of salt
- Fresh mint – 1/2 cup
- Olive oil – 2 tablespoons
- Chopped strawberries – 2 cups

Directions:

1. First of all, skin and chop the cucumbers
2. Chop the strawberries and the fresh mint.
3. Finally add all to a bowl then serve.

211. Herbed Potato Salad

Preparation Time: 10 minutes
Cooking Time: 20 minutes
Servings: 6
Ingredients:

- Red potatoes – 1 ½ pounds
- Brown mustard – ½ tablespoon
- Fresh parsley – 1 tablespoon
- Italian dressing – ½ cup
- Black pepper – ¼ teaspoon
- Garlic salt – 1 teaspoon
- Green bell pepper – ½ cup
- Red bell pepper – ½ cup
- Green onions – ½ cup

Directions:

1. Place the potatoes in a large pot and boil for about 10 minutes. Ensure the potatoes do not become overly soft. Drain off excess water and set aside to cool.
2. Once cool, cut them into small pieces (preferably bite size) and transfer to a medium-sized bowl. Put in a small bowl the Italian dressing, parsley, black pepper and garlic salt. Add the potatoes and mix. With care, stir in green onions, green and red bell peppers. Serve.

212. Corn and Green Chili Salad

Preparation Time: 10 minutes
Cooking Time: 0 minutes
Servings: 4
Ingredients:

- Frozen corn – 2 cups
- Vegetable oil – ½ tablespoon
- Tomatoes – 1 can
- Green chilies – 1 can
- Green onions – 1/3 cup
- Lime juice – 1 tablespoon
- Fresh cilantro – 2 tablespoons

Directions:

1. Place frozen corn, diced tomatoes and chilies in a bowl. Add vegetable oil, lime juice, green onions and cilantro. Mix the ingredients thoroughly. If desired, add diced chicken when serving.

213. Black Bean and Corn Pitas

Preparation Time: 5 minutes
Cooking Time: 1 minutes.
Servings: 4
Ingredients:

- Black beans (low-sodium) – 1 can
- Tomatoes – 1 cup fresh
- Garlic (chopped) – 1
- Frozen corn – 1 cup
- Avocado (chopped) – 1
- Black pepper – 2 teaspoons
- Fresh parsley – 1 teaspoon
- Lemon juice–2 teaspoons
- Whole wheat pita– 2 mediums
- Chili powder – ½ teaspoon
- Mozzarella cheese – 1/3 cup

Directions:

1. Drain the canned black beans and rinse. Combine the beans with tomatoes, garlic, corn and avocado in a medium size bowl. Add cayenne pepper, chili powder, and parsley and lemon juice to the mix in the bowl. Cut the whole wheat pita in half to make 4 pockets.
2. Scoop the fillings into each half of the pita bread. Add cheese as toppings. Serve.

214. Chicken Tortas

Preparation Time: 15 minutes
Cooking Time: 15 minutes
Servings: 4
Ingredients:

- Chicken cooked– 2 cups
- Fresh Tomato sauce – 2 cups
- Chili powder – 1 teaspoon
- Radishes (sliced) – 2
- Romaine lettuce – 2 cups
- Low fat cheese (shredded) – ½ cup
- Avocado (mashed) – 1
- French bread rolls (cut in half) -4

Directions:

1. Combine shredded chicken, a cup of Fresh Salsa and chili powder in a medium-sized bowl. Combine shredded lettuce, cheese, radishes and onion in another medium-sized bowl. On each French bread roll spread an equal amount of avocado. Add the chicken and lettuce mix in equal amounts. Scoop a quarter Fresh Salsa over lettuce already spread on the roll. Close the roll and your sandwich is ready.

215. Avocado Garden Salad

Preparation Time: 10 minutes
Cooking Time: 20 minutes.
Servings: 6
Ingredients:

- Mixed salad vegetables – 6 cups
- Tomatoes chopped – 3
- Cucumber (peeled, chopped) – 1
- Onions (chopped) - 5
- Garlic powder – 1/3 teaspoon
- Lemon juice – 2 tablespoons
- Salt and pepper
- Avocado (peeled) – 1

Directions:

1. Place greens, cucumber, tomatoes and onions in a large bowl and mix together. Mix lemon juice, ground pepper, garlic powder and salt in a small bowl. Pour the lemon juice mix over the salad mix and toss. Prepare the avocado slices: cut into halves, remove pit, peel and slice into wedge-like shapes of about 1/8-inch thickness. Place the avocado slices over the salad. Enjoy!

216. Zesty Asian Chicken Salad

Preparation Time: 5 minutes
Cooking Time: 20 minutes
Servings: 4
Ingredients:

- 3 Chicken breasts boneless and cooked
- Small broccoli florets – ½ cups
- Carrots (peeled, cut in strips) – 2
- Green onions (sliced) – 3
- Red bell pepper (cut in strips) – 1
- Cabbage (shredded) – 2 cups
- Orange juice (100%) – ¼ cup
- Sesame salad dressing
- Fresh cilantro (chopped) – ¼ cup

Directions:

1. Prepare the chicken: cut into tiny strips, and place in a medium-sized bowl. Cook it. Place broccoli florets, red bell pepper, carrots, and cabbage and green onions in the bowl. Mix orange juice and dressing together in a small bowl. Pour the dressing mixture over the salad. Toss until it coats. Add cilantro and stir. Enjoy!

Event and Special Occasion Paleo-Meals

217. Chicken and Sweet Potato Bake

Preparation Time: 15 minutes
Cooking Time: 35 minutes.
Servings: 3 – 4
Ingredients:

- Chicken breasts boneless – 1 lb.
- Broccoli floret – 4 cups
- 1 large sweet potato – cubed
- Red onion – 3 cups, chopped
- Garlic – 2 cloves, minced
- Olive oil – 1/3 cup
- Dried cranberries – ¼ cup
- Salt and pepper to taste
- Italian seasoning – 1 teaspoon

Directions:

1. Preheat your oven to 400°F, and line a baking sheet with a parchment paper. Combine the sweet potato, garlic, broccoli, onion and cranberries on a pain. Sprinkle olive oil over them and add salt and pepper. Toss the ingredients on the pan, and cover with a foil. Put in the oven and allow to it bake for about 12 minutes. Remove from the oven after twelve minutes and add the chicken. Toss and place in the oven. Allow it to bake for about 20 minutes or alternatively, until the chicken is completely cooked, and the potatoes are completely soft. Serve.

218. Apple Turkey Gyro

Preparation Time: 10 minutes
Cooking Time: 25 minutes
Servings: 6
Ingredients:

- Turkey breast – ½ pound
- Apple (cored, sliced) – 1
- Onion (sliced) –1 cup
- Green bell pepper sliced – 2
- Red bell pepper sliced – 2
- Lemon juice – 1 tablespoon
- Vegetable oil – 1 tablespoon
- Whole wheat pita toasted – 6
- Low fat plain yogurt– ½ cup

Directions:

1. Cut the turkey into thin slices. Spray a skillet or a pan with non-stick spraying oil. Stir fry onion, green and red bell peppers and lemon juice in it until they appear crisp and tender.
2. Add the turkey and allow it to cook through. Turn off the heat or remove the pan or skillet from heat. Add apple and stir. Fill a folded pita with the mix. Serve. Drizzle with plain yogurt.

219. Vegetable Quesadillas

Preparation Time: 10 minutes
Cooking Time: 25 minutes
Servings: 4
Ingredients:

- Frozen corn – 1 or 2 cups
- Flour tortillas – 4
- Green onion, sliced – ½
- Green bell pepper chopped – ½
- Tomato chopped – ½
- Cilantro chopped – 2 tablespoons
- Reduced-fat Cheddar – ½ cup
- Non-stick cooking spray

Directions:

1. Spray a medium-sized skillet with the cooking spray and stir fry corn and green pepper in heat over low heat for about 5 minutes. Add chopped tomato and sliced green onion and continue

to cook. Add chopped cilantro when the vegetables have been heated through. Stir frequently.

2. Place tortillas in a large skillet and heat on high. Place the cooked vegetables and cheese in equal amount on each tortilla and fold over. Cook until the cheese melts and the tortillas appear slightly brown and crisp. Serve.

220. Delicious Chicken Curry

Servings: 6
Cooking Time: 1 hour
Ingredients

- 2 pounds chicken meat, chopped
- 2 tablespoons curry
- 2 cups tomato paste
- 1/2 cup heavy cream
- Salt to taste
- 1/2 cup of water
- Cilantro for garnishing

Instructions

1. In a bowl, mix chicken chopped in the curry powder. Add the tomato paste, salt and the cream. Stir to combine. Take a pot add 1/2 cups of water. Stir in and cook on low for 1 hour. Stir often and add water if needed. Serve with cilantro for garnish.

221. Chickpea Curry

Servings: 4
Ingredients

- 3 tablespoons curry
- 4 cups cooked chickpeas
- 1 cup chopped cilantro

Instructions

1. Put all ingredients in the slow cooker and cook on low for 4 hours.

222. Ratatouille

Servings: 6
Ingredients

- 2 large eggplants, sliced
- 2 medium onions, sliced
- 1 red pepper, sliced
- 1 green pepper, sliced
- 4 large tomatoes, sliced
- 2 garlic cloves, sliced
- 4 tablespoons olive oil
- 1 tablespoon fresh basil
- Salt and pepper to taste

Instructions

1. Put all ingredients in the slow cooker and cook on low for 4 hours

223. Eggplant, Zucchini and Tomato

Servings: 4
Cooking Time: 4 hours
Ingredients

- 2 cups sliced zucchini
- 2 cups sliced tomatoes
- 2 tablespoons olive oil
- 2 cups sliced eggplant
- salt and pepper to taste
- ½ tsp. minced garlic

Instructions

1. Arrange all ingredients in the slow cooker dish, cover and cook on low for 4 hours.

224. Menacing Goulash

Preparation Time: 10 minutes   **Cooking Time:** 15 minutes   **Servings:** 4
Ingredients:

- 2 pounds of lean ground beef

- 13 teaspoons of olive oil
- 1 red bell pepper, seeded, chopped
- 1 onion cut up into short strips
- 1 tablespoon of minced garlic
- 2 tablespoons of sweet paprika
- ½ a teaspoon of hot paprika
- 4 cups of beef stock
- 2 cans of petite diced tomatoes

Directions:

1. Take your pot and add 2 teaspoon of olive oil on the bottom. Add the ground beef. Cook it to break it up; once the beef is browned, transfer it to a bowl.
2. Apart from, cut the stem off your pepper, remove the seed and cut it into short strips; cut your onion into short strips. Add extra teaspoon of olive oil, the onions and pepper to your pot.
3. Sauté them for about 3-4 minutes. Add the minced garlic, hot paprika, sweet paprika and cook it for 2-3 minutes. Add the beef stock along with the petite tomatoes. Add the ground beef and close the lid. Allow it to cook for about 15 minutes on low fire. Once it is done, enjoy!

225. Luxurious Rotisserie Chicken

Preparation Time: 5 minutes
Cooking Time: 25 minutes
Servings: 6
Ingredients:

- 1 whole chicken
- 1 ½ teaspoon of salt
- 1 teaspoon of minced garlic
- ½ a teaspoon of pepper
- 1 ½ tablespoon avocado oil
- 1 yellow quartered onion
- 1 halved lemon
- 1 cup of chicken broth

Directions:

1. Remove the parts from your chicken cavity and rinse it well. Pat it dries with a paper towel.
2. Take a pot and add the spices, salt and pepper to it. Stir properly. Add the oil to your spices and stir properly until it mixes fully. Rub the breast with oil and spice the mix. Add the chicken breast and heat it for 5-7 minutes until it gets fully crispy. Flip the breast and crisp the other side for about a minute. Add chicken stock. Cover and cook for 25 minutes. Stir frequently.
3. Turn off the heat, but don't remove the lid for 5-6 minutes. Then, transfer the chicken to your serving plate. Let it rest for 5 minutes and serve by pouring a bit of the cooking liquid on top.

226. Whispering Meal of Lamb

Preparation Time: 10 minutes
Cooking Time: 30 minutes
Servings: 4
Ingredients:

- 2 tablespoons of ghee
- 1 diced onion
- 4 minced garlic cloves
- ½ fresh ginger minced
- 1-2 Serrano peppers minced
- 4 chopped tomatoes
- 1 tablespoon of coriander
- 1 teaspoon of paprika
- Salt and pepper to taste
- ½ a teaspoon of cumin powder
- ½ a teaspoon of chili powder
- ¼ teaspoon of turmeric powder
- 1 pound of ground lamb
- 1 cup of rinsed frozen peas
- 3 chopped carrots
- 2 chopped potatoes
- 1 can of tomato sauce
- Cilantro for garnish

Directions:

1. Take your pot and add the ghee to melt on low. Add the onion and saute them until they get brown thoroughly; then add the garlic, ginger, Serrano pepper and stir properly.
2. Put the tomatoes and cook it for an additional minute. Add the spices and fry it for 1 minute.
3. Place the ground lamb into the pot and cook until it gets fully browned.
4. Add the peas, carrots, tomato sauce, potatoes and mix everything properly. Cover and cook it for about 30 minutes. Stir frequently. If it needs add a bit of water. Turn off the heat but don't remove the lid for 3-4 minutes to allow the heat to release naturally. Serve and enjoy!

227. Succulent Maple Smoked Brisket

Preparation Time: 10 minutes
Cooking Time: 50 minutes
Servings: 5
Ingredients:
- 1 ½ pound of beef brisket
- 2 tablespoons of maple sugar
- Salt and pepper
- 1 teaspoon of mustard powder
- 1 teaspoon of onion powder
- ½ a teaspoon of smoked paprika
- 2 cups of bone broth
- 1 tablespoon of liquid smoke
- 3 fresh thyme sprigs

Directions:
1. Remove the brisket from your fridge for 30 minutes before cooking and pat it dry using paper towels. Take a bowl, add the maple sugar, sea salt, mustard powder, pepper, onion powder, smoked paprika and mix them properly to prepare the spice blender.
2. Take your pot and grease up the bottom using oil. Add the brisket and cook it until it gets brown. Turn the brisket to the fatty side; add the liquid smoke, broth and thyme.
3. Scrape off the browned bits. Cover and cook for about 50 minutes. Stir frequently.
4. Once it is done, turn off the heat, but don't remove the lid to allow the heat to release naturally for 5 minutes. Saute and wait for 10 minutes for the sauce to get thickened. Remove the brisket from the pot and allow it rest. Slice up the brisket; serve it with sauce and whipped veggies.

228. Very Sensual Strawberry Cheesecake

Preparation Time: 10 minutes
Cooking Time: 20 minutes
Servings: 8
Ingredients:
- 2 ounces full fat cream cheese
- 2/3 cup of sugar substitute
- 1 teaspoon of vanilla extract
- 2 eggs at room temperature
- Handful of fresh strawberries
- Strawberry syrup for garnish

Directions:
- Take a Spring Form pan and grease it up properly. Take a mixer and blend your cream cheese until there are no lumps found in it. Add sugar, vanilla extract, to the cream cheese and blend it again. Add the eggs (one at a time) and keep beating the mixture.
- Cover the bottom sides of your pan tightly with one piece of foil. Pour the batter into your Spring Form Pan. Take a pan bigger and add the appropriate amount of water to ensure that the pan is filled by 1-inch. Put the Spring Form Pan into the pan full of water.
- Bake at 300°F for about 30 minutes. Bake other 30 minutes at 120°F.
- Remove the cake to allow it to reach a room temperature. Cover the cake with a plastic wrap and allow it to chill for 5-6 hours in fridge. Serve with your favorite garnish!

229. Chinese Fantastical Turnip Cake

Preparation Time: 25 minutes
Cooking Time: 55 minutes
Servings: 10
Ingredients:

- 2 pieces of Chinese turnip peeled
- 1 ½ pound beef meat chopped
- ¼ cup of dry shrimps soaked up
- 2 tablespoons of olive oil
- 1 teaspoon of minced ginger
- ½ chopped green onion
- 1 ½ teaspoon of salt
- ½ a teaspoon of sugar
- ¼ teaspoon of chicken stock powder
- Half a pack of rice flour
- 1 cup of water
- 2-3 tablespoons of olive oil

Directions:

1. Take a large sized deep pan and heat the olive oil on medium heat. Add the green onion, ginger and sauté it for half a minute. Add the chopped-up beef meat, dry thee shrimp and cook it for 1 minute. Add the shredded Chinese turnips and sauté it for 1-2 minutes. Add the remaining ingredients. Reduce the heat to an average and cover it up. Simmer it for 5 minutes.
2. Take a bowl; add the rice flour and water. Pour the cooked-up turnips mixture and stir properly. Pour the batter into a medium sized Glasslock container.
3. Transfer the mixture to your pot. Add 2 cups of water to your pot.
4. Cover and cook for 45 minutes on medium. Once it is done, turn the heat off but don't remove the lid for 10 minutes to allow the heat to release naturally. Take out the cake and allow it to chill for 2-3 hours. Use a knife and loosen the cake. Flip the cake and take it out. Serve!

230. Living Breathing Rice Pudding

Preparation Time: 5 minutes
Cooking Time: 10 minutes
Servings: 8
Ingredients:

- 1 cup of Arborio rice
- 1 and a ½ cup of water
- ¼ teaspoon of salt
- 2 cups of divided whole milk
- ½ a cup of sugar
- 2 pieces of eggs
- ½ teaspoon of vanilla extract
- ¾ cup of raisins

Directions:

1. Add the rice, the water and salt to your pot. Cover and cook it for about 3 minutes on high heat. After this, turn down the heat and add 1 and a ½ cup of milk with the sugar to your rice. Stir properly. Take a small sized mixing bowl; whisk in the eggs and ½ a cup of milk alongside vanilla. Pour the mixture through a metal mesh into your pot. Simmer until it starts to boil.
2. Turn the heat off and remove the pot. Add the raisins. Let it cool off, as it will thicken the pudding. Serve it warm with toppings of whipped cream, nutmeg or cinnamon. Enjoy!

231. Kid's Favorite Chocolate Fondue

Preparation Time: 2 minutes
Cooking Time: 10 minutes
Servings: 4
Ingredients:

- 3.5 ounces of Swiss Chocolate
- 3 and a ½ ounce of Fresh Cream
- 1 teaspoon of sugar
- 1 teaspoon of Amaretto liquor
- 2 cups of water

Directions:

1. Add 2 cups of water to your pot. Take a small sized heat proof ramekin and add the chocolate chunks. Add the same amount of fresh cream, liquor and sugar. Lower it into your pot.
2. Close the lid and cook it for about 2 minutes on medium heat. Turn off the heat, but don't remove the lid for 5-6 minutes to allow the heat to release naturally. Take it out using tongs or gloves. Stir the contents vigorously for 1 minute. Serve immediately!

232. Ultimate Pan-Fried Lemon Chicken

Preparation Time: 15 minutes
Cooking Time: 15 minutes
Servings: 5
Ingredients:
- Zest and juice of 1 lemon
- Fat of choice
- 1.5 teaspoons olive oil
- Salt and pepper
- 1 chicken breast

Directions:

5. Zest the lemon and squeeze the juice. Add chicken breast, olive oil, lemon zest and juice, salt and pepper to a cooking-zip lock bag. Seal the bag, squeezing out the air.
6. Next, please flatten the chicken with a meat pounder or maybe rolling pin, so it is even in thickness. Set it aside for about 30 to 35 minutes or cook immediately; then add oil or other fat of choice to a skillet and heat over medium-high heat. Remove the chicken from the bag and add to the skillet. Fry the chicken on both sides for about 2 to 5 minutes on each or until cooked. Wait about 5 to 10 minutes before slicing. Serve!

233. Skillet Tuscan Chicken

Preparation Time: 15 minutes
Cooking Time: 30 minutes
Servings: 4
Ingredients:
- 1 lb. chicken breast
- 1 white onion, diced
- 3 cloves garlic, minced
- 5 roasted chopped tomatoes
- 3 sun-dried tomatoes, chopped
- 12 oozes mushrooms, sliced
- 1 tsp. oregano
- ½ tsp. thyme
- Salt and black pepper
- Olive oil

Directions:

1. Heat the olive oil in a large skillet placed over a medium-high heat on the stove top. Add the chicken and sauté for 3 minutes on each side. Remove the chicken, set aside on a plate and cover with aluminum foil to keep warm. Add some more olive oil to the skillet if necessary and then add the sliced mushrooms in a single layer. Sauté for a few minutes per side. Remove from the pan and set aside on a separate plate. Add in the onion and cook until softened for about 4 minutes. Add the sun-dried tomatoes and garlic and sauté for 2-3 minutes.
2. Stir in the diced fire-roasted tomatoes, thyme, oregano, and season with salt and pepper. Put the chicken back into the skillet. Cover and cook until the chicken is fully cooked, about 10-12 minutes. Return the sautéed mushrooms to the pan, combine all well, season and serve!

234. Low Carb and Paleo Asian Chicken Stir Fry

Preparation Time: 5 minutes
Cooking Time: 15 minutes
Servings: 2
Ingredients:
- 2 boneless chicken breasts, chopped
- 2 tbsps. avocado oil

- 1 white onion, diced
- 1 cup pea shoots
- 1 red bell pepper, diced
- 1 zucchini, diced
- ¼ cup garlic, finely minced
- 3 tbsps. coconut aminos
- 1 tsp. lemon juice
- 1 tsp. sesame oil to finish
- Salt and pepper

Directions:
1. Trim any excess fat or tissue from the chicken and cut into chunks and season with salt and pepper. In a large, cast-iron skillet, heat the avocado oil until shimmering on medium high heat.
2. Add the chicken to skillet and cook for 3 minutes until lightly browned. Stir occasionally to prevent burning. Add onion and garlic and stir, continuing to cook until the onions and garlic are soft, fragrant, and lightly brown. This should take another 2-3 minutes. Add in the zucchini and bell peppers and cook until the chicken is golden brown, and the vegetables are softened and lightly caramelized - about 5 minutes. Add the pea shoots, lemon juice, coconut aminos, and sesame oil and toss well over a medium heat for 1-2 minutes. The sauce will thicken slightly and coat the dish evenly. Remove from heat and serve immediately.

235. Cauliflower Beef & Carrot

Servings: 8
Cooking Time: 2 hours 30 minutes
Ingredients
- 2 cup chopped carrots
- 2 cups chopped red onions
- 2 tbsp. olive oil
- 2 cups cauliflower florets
- Salt and pepper
- 2 teaspoons cumin
- 2 cups beef stock
- 4 pounds cubed beef meat

Instructions
1.Put ingredients in the pot. Cover, and cook on low for 2 hours 30 minutes.

236. Pork & Leeks

Servings: 6
Cooking Time: 3 hours
Ingredients
- 1 cup brown rice
- 2 chopped carrot
- 2 tbsp. olive oil
- 3 cups chopped leeks
- Salt and pepper
- 2 cups beef stock
- 4 pounds cubed pork meat

Instructions
1.Put ingredients in the pot. Cover, and cook on low for 3 hours.

237. Eggplant, Tripe & Broccoli

Servings: 4
Cooking Time: 2 hours
Ingredients
- 2 eggplants, sliced
- 2 chopped onions
- 2 cups broccoli
- 1 cup green beans
- 2 tbsp. coconut oil
- Salt and pepper
- 3 bay leaves
- 2 garlic cloves
- 2 cups beef stock
- 4 pounds beef meat, chopped

Instructions

1.Put ingredients in the pot. Cover, and cook on low for 2 hours.

238. Italian Pork & White Beans

Servings: 6
Cooking time: 3 hours
Ingredients

- 2 tomatoes, sliced
- 2 chopped onions
- 2 cups spinach
- 2 cups dried navy beans
- 2 tablespoons olive oil
- Salt and pepper
- 4 bay leaves
- 2 garlic cloves
- 2 cups vegetable stock
- 2 cups water
- 4 pounds pork meat, chopped

Instructions

1.Put ingredients in the pot. Cover, and cook on low for 3 hours.

239. Skillet Shrimp and Spicy Sausage

Preparation Time: 10 minutes   **Cooking Time:** 20 minutes   **Servings:** 4

Ingredients:

- 3 tbsps. extra-virgin olive oil
- 8 oozes shrimp, deveined
- 10 oozes spicy sausage
- 1 medium zucchini, sliced
- 1 medium onion, diced
- 2 large cloves, garlic minced
- 1 green bell pepper, diced
- 1 red bell pepper, diced
- 2 tbsps. tomato paste
- ½ cup chicken broth
- ½ tsp. basil
- ½ tsp. thyme
- ½ tsp. oregano
- ¼ tsp. red pepper flakes
- Pepper and salt, to taste

Directions:

1. Heat a tablespoon of olive oil in a large skillet on a high. Add the peeled shrimp to the skillet and cook until just pink and opaque in the center, stirring for about 5 minutes. Transfer shrimp to a plate and tent with aluminum foil. Add 1 tablespoon of olive oil to the skillet and sauté the onion until soft and translucent. Add the spicy sausage and peppers, cover and cook for about 5 minutes, stirring well. If needed, add another tablespoon of olive oil if the veggies begin to stick to the skillet. Add the zucchini and minced garlic and stir. Then, add the tomato paste and chicken broth, and stir everything well to combine.
2. Season with salt, pepper and all the herbs and spices. Cook for a further 5 - 7 minutes until the sauce is thick and the vegetables tender. Return the shrimp to the skillet and cook for further 3 minutes until all the flavors are fully incorporated.

240. Low Carb Lean Turkey Meatballs

Preparation Time: 10 minutes
Cooking Time: 15 minutes
Servings: 10
Ingredients:

- 1 packet ground turkey
- 1 tbsp. avocado oil or ghee
- ¼ cup almond flour
- 1 egg, lightly beaten
- ½ white onion, chopped
- 2 tsps. dry Italian seasoning
- 1 tsp. garlic powder
- Pepper and salt to taste

Directions:

1. Preheat the oven to 375° Fahrenheit.
2. In a large bowl combine the ground turkey together with all the rest of the ingredients. Combine well but lightly, until everything is mixed in. Using clean hands and an ice cream scoop form 2-inch balls of the mixture into meatballs. Heat the avocado oil or ghee in a large cast iron skillet on medium, then add the meatballs. Brown the meatballs for about 3 minutes, flipping to brown all sides for another 2-3 minutes. Place the skillet with the cooked meatballs directly into oven and bake 15 minutes, until fully cooked. Serve warm.

241. Killet Fudge Brownies

Preparation Time: 10 minutes
Cooking Time: 20 minutes
Servings: 4 servings
Ingredients:

- 1½ teaspoons coconut flour
- 1/3 cup tapioca flour
- 4 tbsps. coconut oil
- 2 tbsps. mashed ripe banana
- 1 cup dark chocolate chips
- 2 eggs
- 1 tsp. vanilla extract
- ¼ tsp. salt
- More chocolate chips for topping

Directions:

1. Preheat the oven to 350° Fahrenheit and grease an 8-inch cast iron skillet with coconut oil.
2. Melt the coconut oil and dark chocolate chips in a medium bowl and stir well to combine.
3. Add the mashed banana, vanilla, and salt and mix together, and whisk in the eggs one at a time.
4. Add both the coconut and tapioca flours and stir until just combined. Be careful not to over mix the batter. Transfer the batter to the skillet, top with additional chocolate chips and bake for 20-22 minutes. The edges will start to pull away from the sides of the skillet and the middle will be just slightly gooey and undercooked. Top with additional chocolate chips and serve.

242. Skillet Moroccan Chicken

Preparation Time: 10 minutes
Cooking Time: 20 minutes
Servings: 2
Ingredients:

- 2 chicken breasts
- ½ tbsp. extra-virgin olive oil
- 2 cups cauliflower, chopped
- ½ cup sweet onion, chopped
- 1 carrot peeled and sliced
- 2 Medjool dates, sliced
- ½ cup cilantro, chopped
- ½ small cucumber, thinly sliced
- ¾ cup fresh orange juice
- ½ cup crushed tomatoes
- 15 roasted pistachios, chopped
- 1½ tsp. fresh ginger, minced
- 1 tsp. ground cinnamon
- 1½ tsp. ground cumin
- ¼ tsp. paprika
- 1/8 tsp. ground allspice
- Salt and pepper, to taste

TO GARNISH:

- Cilantro, chopped

Directions:

1. Using a meat mallet pound the chicken breasts until they are quite flat and season with salt and pepper. Heat the olive oil in a large skillet on a medium-high heat. Cook the chicken until golden brown, about 1-1.5 minutes. Turnover and repeat on the other side and transfer to a plate, tenting

with aluminum foil to keep warm. Lower the heat to medium and add the onion, ginger, carrot, cauliflower, cumin, paprika, cinnamon, and allspice to the pan. Cook for 3 minutes. stirring continuously until the veggies just begin to soften and the spices turn fragrant.

2. Stir in the crushed tomatoes, orange juice, and sliced Medjool dates. Turn the heat up to high and bring the stew and boil for 2 minutes; then lower the heat to medium and simmer for 5 minutes, stirring, until the sauce begins to reduce and thicken. Season to taste.

3. Return the chicken back into the skillet and spoon the sauce over top. Cover and reduce the heat to medium-low and cook until the chicken is no longer pink, for about 10 minutes. Stir in the fresh cilantro and serve the chicken in two plates. Top each serving with chopped pistachios and place the sliced cucumbers on the side. Garnish with extra cilantro and enjoy!

243. One-Pot Steak Potato and Pepper

Preparation Time: 5 minutes
Cooking Time: 50 minutes
Servings: 2-3
Ingredients:

- 1 tbsp. butter
- 1 lb. sirloin steak, chopped
- 1 large Korean yam, chopped

TO GARNISH:

- Chopped fresh cilantro

- 8 yellow/red/green sweet peppers, sliced
- 2 tbsps. extra-virgin olive oil
- 1 small red onion, thinly sliced
- 1 tsp. smoked paprika
- ½ tsp. garlic powder
- Salt and pepper to taste

Directions:

1. Place the butter on the bottom of a large pot and heat on medium until the butter has melted. Swirl the pan so that the butter coats the entire surface. Place all the ingredients into the pot, toss well to combine and cook on medium for 50 minutes. Stir and check frequently to ensure even cooking. Once it is ready, sprinkle with chopped fresh cilantro and serve.

244. Protein-Rich English Breakfast

Preparation Time: 5 minutes
Cooking Time: 30 minutes
Servings: 2
Ingredients:

- 2 eggs
- 4 thinly slices pork meat
- 2 purple sweet potatoes

- 1 tomato
- ½ lb. mushrooms

TO GARNISH:

- Red chili flakes
- Fresh herbs
- Salt and pepper, to taste

Directions:

1. Preheat the oven to 400° Fahrenheit. Take a baking dish with parchment paper. Place the chopped sweet purple potatoes and bake for 15 minutes.

2. In a cast iron skillet, cook on medium the pork meat for 10 minutes. Remove from the skillet, set aside and drain off any extra fat. Slice the tomato and roughly chop the mushrooms. Cook the mushrooms in the same skillet that cooked the meat. When the mushrooms have cooked down, add the tomato slices and cook quickly on high. Remove the mushrooms and tomato slices from the skillet and set onto a plate. Fry the eggs; add a little more oil to ensure they don't stick. Slice

open the sweet potatoes and place them on a plate with the cooked meat, tomato slices, mushrooms, and eggs. Garnish with salt, pepper, herbs, and red chili flakes. Enjoy hot.

245. Delicious Apple Crisp

Preparation Time: 15 minutes
Cooking Time: 30 minutes
Servings: 8
Ingredients:
FOR THE APPLES:

- 6 apples, peeled and sliced thinly
- 2 tbsps. coconut oil
- ¼ cup maple syrup
- ¼ cup water, if needed

- 1 tsp. ground cinnamon
- ½ tsp. ground nutmeg

FOR THE CRUMBLE TOPPING:

- ¼ cup solid coconut oil
- ½ cup unsweetened coconut
- ½ cup walnuts
- ½ cup sliced almonds
- ¼ cup coconut sugar

Directions:

1. Preheat the oven to 350° F.
2. In a cast iron skillet, melt the coconut oil or butter over medium-high heat. Add apples and cook for about 5 minutes, stirring occasionally. Mix in the maple syrup, nutmeg and cinnamon and add a quarter cup of water if mixture turns out dry. Continue to cook for 3-5 minutes, until apples are tender, but not too mushy; then remove from heat and set aside.
3. Meanwhile the in a medium bowl, combine the almonds, walnuts, coconut, and coconut sugar. Stir in the coconut oil until well combined. Sprinkle the crumble over the cooked apples in the skillet. Bake at 350° F for 15-20 minutes or until the topping turns a light golden brown.
4. Serve warm, topped with dairy-free ice cream if desired.

246. Pepper Steak

Servings: 6
Cooking Time: 6 hours
Ingredients

- 2 pounds beef sirloin, chopped
- 1 garlic clove, minced
- 3 tablespoons olive oil

- 2 cups Beef Broth
- ¼ cup tapioca flour
- ½ cup chopped onion
- 2 cups carrots
- 1 cup chopped tomatoes
- Salt

Instructions

1.Sprinkle beef with minced garlic. Heat the oil in a skillet and brown the seasoned beef sirloin strips. Transfer to a pot. Add carrots, onion, chopped tomatoes and salt. Mix in tapioca flour in broth until dissolved. Pour broth into the slow cooker with meat. Cover and cook on medium for 6.

247. Lemon Roast Chicken

Servings: 6
Cooking Time: 6 hours
Ingredients

- 1 whole skinless chicken
- Salt and pepper to taste
- 2 teaspoons Oregano

- 2 garlic cloves minced
- 2 tablespoons olive oil
- 1/2 cup Water
- 3 tablespoons lemon juice
- 1 spring Rosemary, minced

Instructions

1. Add all ingredients to a pot. Cover and cook on low for 6 hours.
2. Add lemon juice when cooking is done and serve!

248. Beef Ratatouille

Servings: 8

Ingredients

- 2 cups sliced zucchini
- 1 chopped onion
- 2 sliced eggplants
- 1 sliced red pepper
- 2 tablespoons olive oil
- 2 garlic cloves, chopped
- Salt and pepper to taste
- 4 pounds cubed beef

Instructions

1. Put ingredients in the pot. Cover, and cook on low for 6 hours.

249. Beef Bourguignonne

Servings 8

Cooking Time: 6 hours

Ingredients

- 4 pounds cubed lean beef
- 1 cup red wine
- 13 tablespoons olive oil
- 1 spring thyme, minced
- Salt and pepper to taste
- 2 garlic cloves, minced
- 1 onion, diced
- 1-pound mushrooms, sliced
- 1/2 cup tapioca flour

Instructions

1.Marinate beef in wine, oil, thyme and pepper for 3 hours at room temperature. Add beef with marinade and all other ingredients to a pot. Cook on low for 6 hours.

250. Tasty Chicken

Servings 6

Cooking time: 6 hours

Ingredients

- 1 whole skinless chicken
- 1/4 cup almond flour
- Salt and pepper to taste
- 1/2 cup chicken broth
- 1/2 cup sliced mushrooms
- 1 teaspoon paprika
- 2 zucchinis, chopped
- Parsley to garnish

Instructions

1.Season chicken with 1 tsp. salt. Combine flour, pepper, remaining salt, and paprika. Coat chicken pieces with this mixture. Place zucchini first in a crockpot. Pour broth over zucchini. Arrange chicken on top. Cover and cook on low for 6 hours. Turn control to high, add mushrooms, cover, and cook on high for additional 10-15 minutes. Garnish with parsley and pepper.

21-Day Meal Plan

Day	Breakfast	Lunch	Snacks/Desserts	Dinner
1	Morning Scramble	Okra and Beef Stew	Kale Crisps	Jalapeno Guacamole
2	Pinnacle Dark Chocolate Mousse	Paleo Basil Avocado Chicken Salad	Sugar Snap Bacon	Asian Stir Fry Bacon
3	King sized Waffles For Lunch Recipe	Beef Broth	Sweet Potato Pancake	Vintage Canned Tuna Ceviche
4	Chipotle Beef Lettuce Wraps	Excellent Tomatoes ad Avocado Omelets	Awesome Spiced Orange Glazed Ham	Best Chicken with Mushroom Sauce
5	Charming Blueberry Lemon Muffins	Very Heartwarming Egg Roll Soup	Cucumber Tomato Salad	Omelet With Avocado And Pico De Gallo
6	Lucky Quinoa Veggie Breakfast Bowl	Cilantro Garlic Pork chop	Berry Delicious smoothie	Mighty Paleo Crock Pot Beef Stew
7	Vintage Zucchini and Sweet Potato (Fritatta)	Magical Beef Short Ribs For Paleo Lovers	Perfect Berry Delicious Smoothie	King sized Cherry-Berry Medley
8	Best Butternut Squash and Kale Beef Stew	Fantastic Nori salmon handroll	Rich Omelet Under Applesauce	Crazy Bacon wrapped sausages
9	Fried Queso Blanco	Porcini and Tomato Glazing Beef Ribs	Titanic Apple Butter	Hot sauce Lamb
10	Mighty Spicy Red Fish Stew	Iconic Simple Zucchini Fritters	Tasty Palo Delicious Zucchini Smoothie	Beef Meatballs and White Beans
11	Breakfast Paleo Burrito	Delightful Mexican Meatloaf	Yummy Kale Omelett	Vegetarian Chili
12	Crazy Paleo Chili Turkey Stew	Super Paleo Mexican Beef Stew	Unique Banana Pancakes	Coolest Beef Bourguignon
13	Delightful Double Chocolate Cookies	Curried Chicken Salad	King-sized Cherry Berry Medley	Spinach with Bacon and Shallots
14	Perfect Scotch eggs	Fantastic Nori salmon handroll	Pan-fried Lemon Chicken	Pinnacle Summer veggie Surprise
15	Dashing Garlic Mushrooms	Great Amazing Eggplant Dip	Awesome Safe Blueberry Muffin	Roasted Brussels Sprouts and Bacon
16	Happy Delicious Glazed carrots	Lamb Pecan salad	Baked Tortillas	Super Paleo Slow Cooker Fajita Soup
17	Charming Lemon Thyme Lamb Chops	Authentic Kalua Pork With A Secret Twist	Delightful Almond Butter Cups	Hillbilly Cheese Surprise
18	Fantastic Gingersnaps	Best Cuban Picadillo	Chocolate Granola	Beef Taco Soup
19	Funny Sautéed Kale	Pork Meat Stew	Crazy Almond Joy Ice Cream	Quick Eggs Benedict On Artichoke Hearts
20	Scrumptious Crispy Sea Bass	Grain Free Balls With Sauce	Super Peach Granita Almondine	Green Beans and Almonds
21	Great Garlic Mushrooms with Bacon	Clean and Simple Meatball	Shrimp Avocado Salad	Pork chop with Greek Salsa

Conclusion

Thank you for reading this book!

I hope this is not only a usual cookbook that you will forget about after a short time, but a guide allows you to have healthier and more time for yourself!

Enjoy your delicious meals!

I wish you to achieve all your goals!

Simon James

CPSIA information can be obtained
at www.ICGtesting.com
Printed in the USA
BVHW011518100321
602204BV00005B/253